CROCHET
for babies and toddlers

CROCHET
for babies and toddlers

Betty Barnden

NEW HOLLAND

Reprinted in 2010
First published in 2002 by
New Holland Publishers (UK) Ltd
London · Cape Town · Sydney · Auckland

Garfield House, 86-88 Edgware Road, London W2 2EA, United Kingdom
www.newhollandpublishers.com

80 McKenzie Street, Cape Town 8001, South Africa

Unit 1, 66 Gibbes Street, Chatswood, NWSW 2067, Australia

218 Lake Road, Northcote, Auckland, New Zealand

ISBN 978-1-85974-996-8

Designer: Frances de Rees
Photographer: John Freeman
Pattern Checker: Sue Whiting
Diagrams: Steve Dew
Illustrations: Moira McTague
Technical Illustrations: Carrie Hill
Editorial Direction: Rosemary Wilkinson
Editor: Clare Hubbard
Assistant Editor: Emily Preece-Morrison

Reproduction by Pica Digital PTE Ltd, Singapore
Printed and bound in Malaysia by Times Offset (M) Sdn. Bhd.

CONTENTS

INTRODUCTION

With a ball or two of yarn and a simple hook you can create pattern and texture in any shape. A few basic stitches, once learnt, can be combined in many ways to form beautiful stitch patterns and motifs. Traditionally, crochet work used very fine hooks and cotton or linen threads to make intricate patterns in imitation of handmade lace for articles such as collars, cuffs and tablecloths. The related technique of Tunisian or Afghan crochet used heavier woollen yarns to create firm, warm fabrics for blankets and coats. While these traditions continue, crochet today also takes advantage of current ranges of knitting yarns, combining colour and texture to create easy-to-wear, practical fabrics suitable for all types of garments as well as blankets, toys and other articles.

Designs in this book include simple, quickly-made garments suitable for beginners, such as the Two Easy Jumpers and the Striped Jumper (with Rabbit), and more complicated and challenging designs such as the Christening Shawl and the Two-Colour Jumper. The detailed instructions for each design are accompanied by measurement diagrams and a stitch diagram illustrating with symbols the main stitch/stitches used. Actual measurements for each garment are given with the sizes, so you can choose which size will best suit your needs. If in doubt, make a larger size.

The basic crochet stitches used in the designs are described in detail along with tips for making up and finishing. Various special techniques are covered, including Intarsia (used for the Polar Bear Jacket and the Sleeping Bag), Woven Crochet (Tartan Cropped Jacket and Beret) and Filet Crochet (Rabbit Curtain). Appliqué motifs such as flowers, stars and snowflakes can be used to decorate any garment. For example, you could personalize your design by stitching little flower motifs from the Pinafore onto the Lacy Cardigan, or a rabbit motif from the Nursery Cushion onto the Bib Pants.

Whether you are making a practical outfit for a new baby or a gift for a special occasion such as a christening or birthday, there's a whole range of designs and items from which to choose. I hope you will enjoy making these designs as much as your family and friends will enjoy receiving and using them.

SUBSTITUTING YARNS

If you cannot obtain the yarn specified for a pattern, try to find an alternative of the same weight and fibre content. "Fingering" yarns are likely to be equivalent to 3-ply or 4-ply. "Sport" or "Worsted" may often be substituted for DK (double knitting). Be sure to check your tension with the new yarn very carefully if you are making a garment; for toys and other accessories the finished size is not so crucial. For larger projects, it is a good idea to buy just one ball of substitute yarn and try to obtain the correct tension before buying all the yarn. The amount of substitute yarn required may vary from the amount quoted in the pattern.

TECHNIQUES

Yarns

Most of the designs in this book are worked in knitting yarns particularly suited to babies' and children's garments, being machine-washable, soft and non-irritating to sensitive skins. Other yarns used are natural fibres such as cotton and silk, with a smooth, soft finish. If possible, always use the brand of yarn specified in the instructions. Stockist information appears on page 112.

Hooks

Crochet hooks are now manufactured in a range of international sizes measured in millimetres (mm). Previously, size ranges made in Europe, the UK and USA did not directly correspond, so instructions could be confusing, and substitution very difficult. Therefore this book quotes only international sizes in millimetres.

Smaller sizes of hooks are normally made of aluminium and larger sizes of plastic, wood or bamboo. They must be smooth with no nicks or scratches, so it is worth replacing old hooks from time to time.

Crochet hooks are manufactured in a range of sizes and are usually made from aluminium, plastic, wood or bamboo.

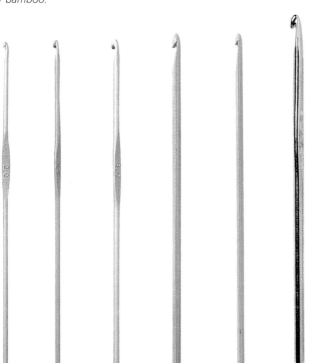

FIRST STEPS
Holding the hook and yarn
For practising, use a fairly substantial yarn such as double knitting, with an appropriate hook, such as size 4.00 mm. If you are left handed, try propping up the book next to a mirror, so you can read the text and look at the illustrations in reverse.

You may hold the hook in one of two ways, whichever you find the most natural: hold it as you would a pencil (fig. 1) or as you would a knife (fig. 2). Place the ball of yarn to your left.

Make a chain (abbreviation: ch)
1 First make a slip knot about 10 cm (4 in) from the beginning of the yarn: make a loop and use the hook to draw another loop through it (fig. 3). Gently tighten the knot and slide it up to the hook (fig. 4).

2 The left hand holds the work and controls the yarn. There are several ways to hold the yarn with the fingers, but this method gives good control: wrap the yarn round the little finger to stop it slipping, then over the index finger, which can then control the position of the yarn relative to the hook (fig. 5).

3 Hold the slip knot between the thumb and middle finger of the left hand, use the hook to catch the yarn next to the index finger and pull a loop through the slip knot, so making a new loop on the hook (fig. 6). 1 chain made. Do not pull too tightly.

4 Always holding the work close to the hook, repeat step 3 to length required (fig. 7). All the chains should be the same size and not too tight.

5 To fasten off, cut the yarn about 10 cm (4 in) from the hook and pull the yarn end through the last loop on the hook.

1
2

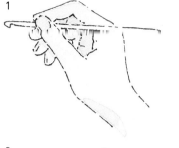

3

4

5

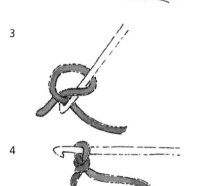

6

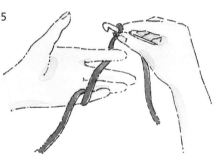

7

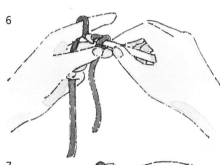

BASIC STITCHES

Stitches worked in rows usually begin with a base chain of a specific number of stitches. Do not count the slip knot as the first chain or the loop on the hook as a chain. It is best to count the chains as you make them, then lay the work flat (without twisting) and count them again.

When working into a base chain, you may insert the hook either under the single top thread of each chain, or under the top two threads of each chain (which is sometimes easier to see). Decide which method is easier for you and be consistent.

When you reach the end of a row turn the work clockwise to prevent twisting the edge stitches.

Try out these basic stitches beginning with a base chain of about 20 ch:

Double crochet (abbreviation: dc)

row 1: insert hook in 2nd ch from hook, wrap yarn round hook (fig. 1) and pull a loop of yarn through this ch (2 loops on hook). Wrap yarn round hook again (fig. 2) and pull another loop through both loops on hook. 1 dc made (fig. 3). Work 1 dc in each ch to end (do not work into the slip knot), turn the work.

row 2: 1 ch, insert hook under 2 threads at top of first dc (fig. 4) and work 1 dc, then work 1 dc in each dc to end of row. Turn. Repeat row 2. There should be the same number of dc on each row.

1

2

3

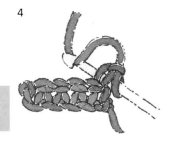

4

The 1 ch at beginning of each row is called a turning chain. Different stitches require different numbers of turning chain, as given below.

When working rows of dc, always begin each row in the first dc and do not work into the turning chain at the end. Do not count the turning chain as a stitch.

Half treble (abbreviation: htr)

row 1: wrap yarn round hook in the direction shown and insert hook in 3rd ch from hook (fig. 5), pull a loop of yarn

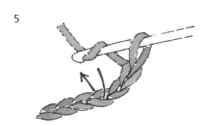

5

through this ch only (3 loops on hook) and wrap yarn round hook again (fig. 6). Pull this loop through all 3 loops on hook (fig. 7). 1 htr made. Work 1 htr in each ch to end, turn the work.

row 2: 2 ch, insert hook under 2 threads at top of first htr and work 1 htr, then work 1 htr in each htr to end of row, turn. Repeat row 2.

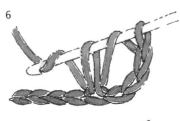

6

7

Treble (abbreviation: tr)

row 1: wrap yarn round hook in the direction shown and insert hook in 4th ch from hook (fig. 8), pull a loop of yarn through this ch only (3 loops on hook) and

8

9

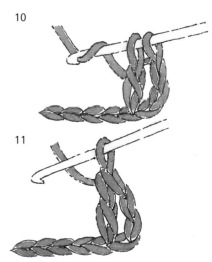

10

11

wrap yarn round hook again (fig. 9). Pull this loop through the first 2 loops on hook and wrap yarn round hook again (fig. 10). Pull this loop through the remaining 2 loops on hook (fig. 11). 1 tr made. Work 1 tr in each ch to end, turn the work.

row 2: 3 ch, miss first tr of previous row, insert hook under two threads at top of next tr and work 1 tr in each tr, ending with 1 tr in 3rd of 3 ch at beginning of previous row, turn.

Repeat row 2.

Depending on the yarn, hook and firmness of fabric required, rows of trebles are sometimes worked with two turning chains instead of three for a neater edge. Always follow the instructions in any particular pattern or shaping may be affected. The two or three turning ch are usually counted as the first stitch of the row.

Always work the first treble of a row into the second treble of the previous row, and always work the last treble of a row into the top of the turning chain at the beginning of the previous row.

OTHER COMMON STITCHES
Double treble (abbreviation: dtr)

Wrap yarn twice round hook, insert hook as directed, wrap yarn round hook, pull this loop through work only (4 loops on hook), wrap yarn round hook, pull this loop through first 2 loops on hook, wrap yarn round hook, pull this loop through next 2 loops on hook, wrap yarn round hook, pull this loop through remaining 2 loops on hook. 1 dtr made.

Slip stitch (abbreviation: ss)

Insert hook as directed, wrap yarn around hook, pull this loop through work and through loop on hook in one movement. 1 ss made.

This is a very short stitch used to close a ring of chain or a round of crochet. Sometimes it is used to work along the edge of a piece to take the yarn to another position without adding any bulk to the fabric.

Most stitch patterns in this book are combinations of the above stitches. Other stitches used are described as they occur.

TO FASTEN OFF

At the end of a piece, work 1 ch, cut yarn at least 10 cm (4 in) from the work and pull through the last chain. Longer ends may be left if required for making up.

To fasten off when working in rounds, work the last slip stitch as given and cut the yarn leaving an end of at least 10 cm (4 in) and pull the cut end through the work. Insert the hook in the same place, from the back of the work through to the front, catch the cut end and pull it through to the wrong side.

TENSION

It is most important to check your tension before beginning to work from any pattern. Tension varies not only with the yarn and hook size used, but also with the hands of the individual crocheter. The numbers of stitches and rows given in any crochet pattern have been carefully calculated according to the tension quoted in that pattern, so if your tension is too loose your work will be too big, and if your tension is too tight your work will be too small. A difference of just 1 stitch in 10 cm (4 in) can give a variation of several centimetres or inches over a whole garment.

Each design in this book recommends a tension for the main stitch used. Using the yarn and hook size given, work a sample piece at least 15 cm (6 in) square. Press the sample as instructed on the yarn ball band. When working with acrylic yarn it is advisable to leave the sample for a few hours or overnight before measuring the tension – measurements may vary as the yarn relaxes.

Lay the sample on a flat surface and insert two pins 10 cm (4 in) apart along a straight row of stitches and away from the edges of the sample, measuring with a ruler or tape measure (fig. 1). Count the number of stitches between the pins. Then insert two pins 10 cm (4 in) apart, one above the other, and count the number of rows between them (fig. 2).

If your work has more stitches or rows than the given tension, your tension is too tight and you should make another sample piece with a larger hook size.

TIPS

● Some balls of yarn may be unwound by pulling the thread out from the centre, which prevents the ball from rolling around as you work. Yarn supplied wound onto a cardboard (or other) centre may be pulled out from a small plastic bag, loosely closed with an elastic band, to prevent soiling.

● Always join in a new ball of yarn at the beginning of a row, never in the middle. To avoid having to unravel the work, try this technique: when you think you have enough yarn left for two rows, tie a loose slip knot at the centre of the remaining yarn and work one row. If you have to unpick the knot, there isn't enough yarn left for another row.

● Count stitches, rows and rounds carefully. Plastic coil rings are available in various sizes and colours to use as markers (fig. 3) or you can use short lengths of contrasting yarn tied into loops. When working several repeats of rows, for example on a sleeve shaping, it is a good idea to make a note of each row as you complete it.

3

● When working two matching pieces such as sleeves to a given length, make a note of the number of rows worked on the first piece, then make the second piece exactly the same.

● When measuring the length as work progresses, lay it on a flat surface and measure at the centre, not at a side edge.

● When working with dark colours it can be difficult to see the stitches, especially by artificial light. Try a daylight bulb in a desk lamp and cover your knees with a white cloth.

1

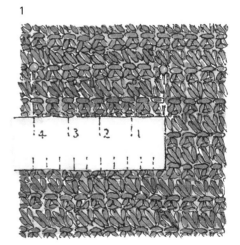

2

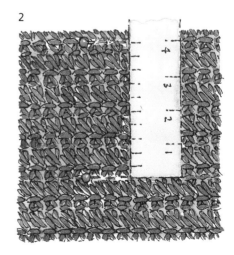

If your work has less stitches or rows than the given tension, your tension is too loose and you should try again with a smaller hook size.

MAKING UP

Always use a blunt-ended needle (sold as a tapestry needle or knitter's making-up needle) to avoid splitting the yarn. These needles are available in various sizes to suit different thicknesses of yarn.

As a rule, sew with the yarn used for the garment, to avoid problems when the garment is washed. Thick yarns will sometimes split into two thinner threads, or you can use a finer matching yarn of the same fibre content.

Seams on baby garments should not be lumpy or bulky. This method is neat and presses flat:

Woven flat seam

Hold the two pieces to be joined with right side together and the left forefinger between them as shown. Insert the needle from the front through both pieces just below corresponding stitches and pull it through to the back. Insert the needle from the back through both pieces just below the next pair of corresponding stitches and pull it through to the front (fig. 1). Make each stitch quite small; to join rows of double crochet work about 1 stitch per row, for rows of trebles work 2 or 3 stitches per row. Match the ends of the rows carefully. Draw the yarn quite tightly for a neat finish. Press the seam open following the instructions on the ball band.

1

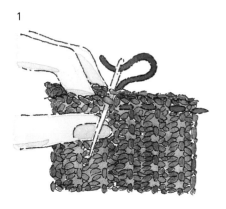

Yarn ends

These should never be secured with a knot. Use a blunt-ended needle to run them in either along the back of a row of stitches or along the wrong side of a seam line, for at least 5 cm (2 in), then trim off the excess yarn.

When working a border it is often possible to work over any yarn ends enclosing them within the border stitches for at least 5 cm (2 in). After completing the border pull gently on the yarn ends to tighten them and trim off the excess.

Buttons and fastenings

It is best to purchase buttons after completing a garment to make sure they fit the buttonholes snugly. Many of the fancy shaped buttons available are not really suitable for crochet (or knitted) garments because they are liable to catch on the yarn. Choose smooth, round buttons.

Lay the garment on a flat surface and lap the buttonhole band over the button band, matching the edges and pattern exactly. Insert pins at right angles to the button band level with the centre of each buttonhole. Sew a button at each marked position, at the centre of the button band, using the same yarn as the garment or matching sewing thread.

Plastic press fasteners are more suitable than metal for baby garments. Sew them on with matching sewing thread, taking 4 or 5 tiny stitches through each hole round the edge of each half.

Pressing

Washing and pressing instructions are normally printed on yarn ball bands. Don't throw all the ball bands away! File one for future reference.

As a general guide:

Natural fibres (wool, cotton, silk) may be pressed under a damp cloth with a warm iron. Do not overpress textured patterns.

Man-made fibres may be pressed under a dry cloth with a moderate or cool iron. Some require no pressing at all. If in doubt, use your tension sample as a test piece.

It is a good idea to make a collection of all your tension samples with a ball band of the yarn used attached to each one.

Embroidery

Simple embroidery is used to decorate some of the designs in this book. Use a blunt-ended needle to avoid splitting stitches and work quite loosely so the work remains flat.

1

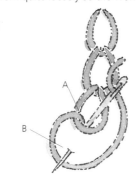

CHAIN STITCH (fig.1)
Bring thread out at A and hold down with left thumb. Insert needle back in same hole and bring the point out a short distance

away at B. Pull thread through, keeping loop under needle point. Repeat to length of chain required and end with a small stitch to secure the last loop.

2

SINGLE CHAIN STITCH (fig.2)
This stitch, sometimes called Lazy Daisy Stitch, is worked in the same way as Chain Stitch, securing each loop with a small stitch.

3

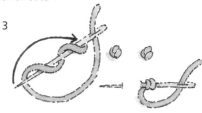

FRENCH KNOT (fig.3)
Bring needle out at front. Wind yarn round it twice, then hold thread down with left thumb and insert needle close to where it emerged. Pull thread through to the back. Repeat as required.

4

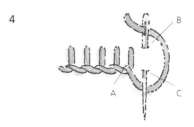

BLANKET STITCH (fig.4)
Work from left to right. Bring needle out at A. * Hold thread down with left thumb and insert needle at B, bringing it out at C, over the loop of thread. Pull needle through and repeat from * as required.

*Embroidery on
Strawberry Jumper*

WORKING IN ROUNDS

Sometimes crochet is not worked back and forth in rows, but in rounds.

Flat geometric shapes (circles, squares, hexagons) begin at the centre with a small ring of chain stitch (fig.1). Each round is normally worked anti-clockwise with right side of work facing, beginning with a number of chain as a substitute for the first stitch and ending with a slip stitch into one of these chain to close the round.

1

Bowl shapes such as hats are also worked in rounds to avoid seams. Depending on the stitch used, the rounds may be worked in a continuous spiral to keep the pattern uniform all over. For accuracy place a stitch marker on the first stitch of each round, moving it up from round to round as work proceeds. Cuffs and borders are often worked in rounds to make neat edges.

WORKING FROM CHARTS
Intarsia

This is a method of working a design from a chart in two or more colours, using a separate ball of yarn for each area of colour. Colours are never passed across the back of the work from one area to another. The chart shows the right side of the work and each small square (or rectangle) represents one stitch. Begin at the bottom of the chart and read right side rows (odd numbers) from right to left and wrong side rows (even numbers) from left to right. Count the stitches carefully and change colours where required as follows:

To change colours in trebles

Begin the last stitch in the old colour: yarn round hook, insert hook, pull through, yarn round hook, pull through first two loops on hook, change to new colour, yarn round hook, pull new colour through 2 loops on hook (fig.2). Leave old colour at wrong side.

2

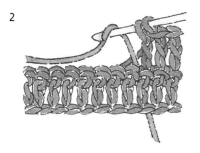

To change colours in half trebles

Begin the last stitch in the old colour: yarn round hook, insert hook, pull old colour through, change to new colour, yarn round hook, pull new colour through 3 loops on hook. Leave old colour at wrong side of work.

On subsequent rows the old colour may not be in exactly the right position for the colour change. If the new colour change comes before the old colour change, the required colour may be loosely stranded across a few stitches and this 'float' caught down later when running in the ends. If the interval is more than a few stitches it is best to cut the yarn and rejoin it in the new position otherwise the work may be pulled out of shape.

If the new colour change comes after the old colour change, stitches may be worked over the required colour to enclose it and bring it to the new position. Note that this should only be done along the outline of the design otherwise the enclosed colour is likely to show through.

Filet crochet

This technique uses a regular mesh pattern with certain squares filled to form the design. Each square on a Filet Crochet chart represents not one single stitch, but either a mesh square or a block. A typical mesh square might be formed by working 1 ch, miss 1 st, 1 tr in next st and a block by working 1 tr in each of next 2 sts.

Begin at the bottom of the chart and read right side rows (odd numbers) from right to left and wrong side rows (even numbers) from left to right. For each row, work the turning chain given, then work each square on the chart as either a mesh square or a block.

COMMON ABBREVIATIONS

ch – chain; col – colour; cont – continue; cm – centimetres; beg – beginning; dc – double crochet; dtr – double treble; foll – following; htr – half treble; in – inches; lp – loop; patt – pattern; rep – repeat; RS – right side; sp – space; ss – slip stitch; st(s) – stitch(es); tog – together; tr – treble; WS – wrong side; yrh – yarn round hook.
2 dc tog – 2 double crochet together = [insert hook in next st, yrh, pull through a loop] twice, yrh, pull through all loops on hook.
3 dc tog – 3 double crochet together = as 2 dc tog but rep [ ] 3 times in all.
2 htr tog – 2 half trebles together = [yrh, insert hook in next st, pull through a loop] twice, yrh, pull through all loops on hook.
3 htr tog – 3 half trebles together = as 2 htr tog but repeat [ ] 3 times in all.
2 tr tog – 2 trebles together = [yrh, insert hook in next st, yrh, pull through a loop, yrh, pull through 2 loops] twice, yrh, pull through all loops on hook.
3 tr tog – 3 trebles together = as 2 tr tog but rep [ ] 3 times in all.

STITCH DIAGRAMS

Each pattern in this book is accompanied by one or more Stitch Diagrams representing the main stitch patterns used in a visual form, intended as an addition to the written instructions, which should always be read carefully.

Key to Stitch Diagrams (fig.3).

Note that symbols may be squashed or stretched to fit the diagrams.

3

⬯	CHAIN
•	SLIP STITCH
+	DOUBLE CROCHET
T	HALF TREBLE
⊤	TREBLE
⧧	DOUBLE TREBLE

Stitches worked in the same place are shown joined at the base.

e.g. = 2 half trebles into 1 chain

Two or more stitches worked together are shown joined at the top

e.g. = 3 trebles together

PATTERN NOTES

1 Figures in brackets ( ) refer to the larger sizes. Where only one set of figures is given this refers to all sizes.
2 Instructions in square brackets [ ] should be positioned together as given, or repeated the number of times given after the brackets.
3 Use one set of measurements throughout: choose either metric (cm) or imperial (in). Do not mix instructions for the two sets of measurements.

WRAPOVER TOP, SHORTS AND HAT

A PRACTICAL YET BEAUTIFUL OUTFIT FOR ANY NEW BABY: EASY TO PUT ON, SOFT AND WARM TO WEAR.

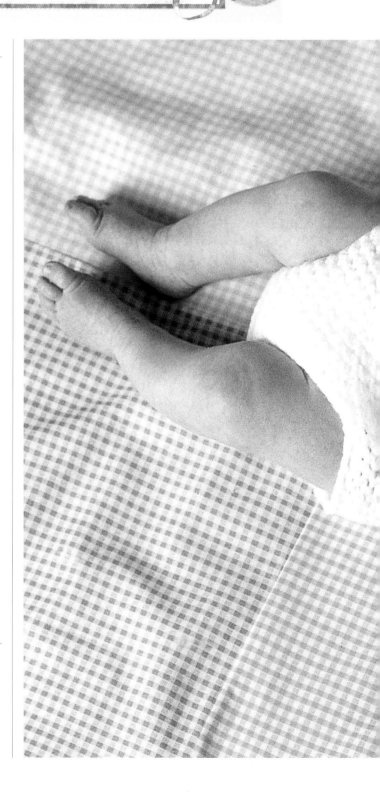

SIZES (see also page 16)

TOP			
to fit chest	31	36	41 cm
	12	14	16 in
actual measurement	36	41	47 cm
	14	16	18¼ in
length to shoulder	19	21.5	24 cm
	7½	8½	9½ in
sleeve seam	9.5	11.5	13.5 cm
	3¾	4½	5¼ in
SHORTS			
to fit hips	31	36	41 cm
	12	14	16 in
HAT			
to fit head	38	40.5	43 cm
	15	16	17 in

MATERIALS

3 (3, 3) x 50 g balls of Patons Fairytale 3-ply (for the set) in col.3300 Snow White
2.00 mm and 2.50 mm hooks
2 popper fasteners or 1 m (3 ft) narrow ribbon for top
shirring elastic and 3 popper fasteners for shorts

TENSION
TOP AND SHORTS: 12 patterns and 19 rows to 10 cm (4 in) measured over Between Stitch as below, using size 2.50 mm hook.
HAT: First 4 rounds should measure 4 cm (1½ in) in diameter.

Special Abbreviation: 2 htr tog: yrh, insert hook in next sp as given in pattern, yrh, pull through a lp, yrh, insert in foll sp, yrh, pull through a lp, yrh, pull through 5 lps on hook.

WRAPOVER TOP

NOTE
For minimal seams, the body is worked in one piece up to the armholes and the yoke is worked in one piece across the body and sleeves.

SLEEVES (make 2)
Using size 2.50 mm hook make 29 (33, 37) ch.

row 1 (RS row): 2 htr in 3rd ch from hook, * miss 1 ch, 2 htr in next ch, rep from * to end, turn. 14 (16, 18) patts.

Between Stitch

row 2: 2 ch, * miss 2 htr, 2 htr in sp before next 2 htr, rep from * ending 2 htr under 2 ch at beg previous row, turn.
Rep this row twice more. 4 rows in all.

Shape Sleeve

row 5: 3 ch, 2 htr in 3rd ch from hook, patt as set to end, turn.
row 6: as row 5. 16 (18, 20) patts.
rows 7 & 8 (7–10, 7–12): rep row 2, 2 (4, 6) times in all.
Rep rows 5–8 (5–10, 5–12), once more, and rows 5 & 6 once again.
20 (22, 24) patts. 14 (18, 22) rows in all.

BETWEEN STITCH

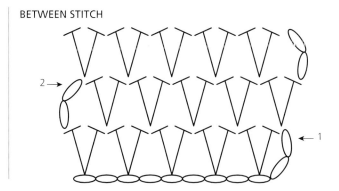

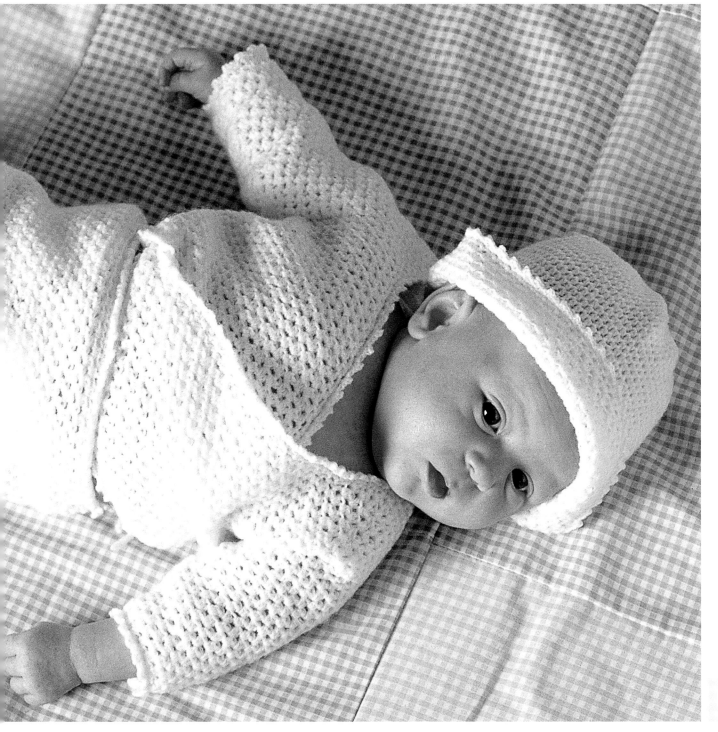

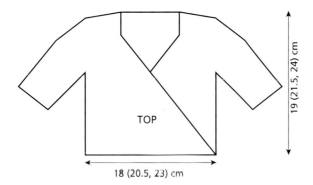

TOP

19 (21.5, 24) cm

18 (20.5, 23) cm

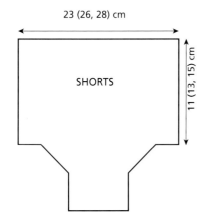

23 (26, 28) cm

SHORTS

11 (13, 15) cm

Rep row 2, 3 more times. 17 (21, 25) rows in all, ending with a RS row. Fasten off.

BODY

Using size 2.50 mm hook make 129 (149, 169) ch.
Work row 1 as for Sleeves. 64 (74, 84) patts.

Shape Front Edges

row 2: 2 ch, miss 2 htr, 1 htr in next sp (counts as first patt), *
miss 2 htr, 2 htr in next sp, rep from * ending 1 htr in last sp, 1 htr
under 2 ch at beg previous row (last 2 htr count as last patt), turn.
63 (73, 83) patts.
Rep this row 19 (21, 23) more times. 44 (52, 60) patts. 21 (23, 25)
rows in all, ending with a RS row. Do not fasten off but continue:

YOKE

row 1: 2 ch, miss 2 htr, 1 htr in next sp, 8 (10, 12) patts as set, then
with WS of first sleeve facing work across top edge: miss first 4 htr,
2 htr in next sp, 16 (18, 20) patts as set leaving 4 htr at end.
Continue along top edge of Body: miss next 8 htr, 2 htr in next sp,
18 (22, 26) patts as set, then work across top edge of second sleeve
in same way as first. Continue along top edge of Body: miss next
8 htr, 2 htr in next sp, 7 (9, 11) patts as set, 1 htr in last sp, 1 htr
under 2 ch at beg previous row, turn. 71 (83, 95) patts.
row 2: 2 ch, miss 2 htr, 1 htr in next sp, * patt as set to sp between
body and sleeve, 1 htr in this sp, rep from * 3 more times, patt as
set ending 1 htr in last sp, 1 htr under 2 ch, turn.
row 3: 2 ch, miss 2 htr, 1 htr in next sp, * patt as set to sp before
single htr, 2 htr tog over this sp and next sp, rep from * 3 more
times, patt as set ending 1 htr in last sp, 1 htr under 2 ch, turn.
row 4: 2 ch, miss 2 htr, 1 htr in next sp, * patt as set to sp before
2 htr tog, 2 htr tog over this sp and next sp, rep from * 3 more
times, patt as set ending 1 htr in last sp, 1 htr under 2 ch, turn.

Rep row 4, 2 (4, 6) more times.
next row: decrease at armhole positions only: 2 ch, miss 2 htr, *
patt as set to sp before 2 htr tog, 2 htr tog over this sp and next sp,
rep from * 3 more times, patt as set ending 2 htr in last sp, 2 htr
under 2 ch, turn.
Rep this row 5 more times.
next row: 2 ch, * 2 htr tog over next 2 sps, patt as set to sp before
2 htr tog, rep from * twice, 2 htr tog over next 2 sps, 2 htr under
2 ch, turn.
foll row: 2 ch, * 2 htr tog over next 2 sps, patt as set to sp before
next 2 htr tog, rep from * twice, 2 htr tog over last sp and under
2 ch. Fasten off.
Join sleeve and underarm seams.

CUFFS (make 2)

With RS of Sleeve facing, using size 2.00 mm hook, join yarn at base
of sleeve seam.
round 1: 1 ch, 1 dc in base of each ch all round, ending 1 ss in 1 ch
at beg of round.
round 2: * 2 ch, 1 ss in st at base of these 2 ch (a picot made), 1 dc
in each of next 2 dc, rep from * all round, ending 1 ss in base of
2 ch at beg of round. Fasten off.

FRONT, NECK AND LOWER EDGE BORDER

With RS of work facing, using size 2.00 mm hook, join yarn at lower
edge below one sleeve.
round 1: 1 ch, 1 dc in base of each ch to corner, 4 dc in same place
at corner, 3 dc in side edge of every 2 rows up front edge, 1 dc in
each htr along neck edge, working 2 dc tog at each corner of back
neck; 3 dc in side edge of every 2 rows down front edge to corner,
4 dc in same place at corner, 1 dc in base of each ch ending 1 ss in
1 ch at beg of round.
round 2: work as round 2 of cuff, with 1 extra picot at each
front corner.

TO FINISH

Fronts may be overlapped in either direction, as required. Sew on
poppers at corners to fasten, or stitch ribbon ties, length approx.
25 cm (10 in), as desired.
Press as instructed on ball bands.

SHORTS

BACK

Using size 2.50 mm hook make 21 (23, 25) ch.
row 1: 2 htr in 3rd ch from hook, * miss 1 ch, 2 htr in next ch, rep
from * to end, turn. 10 (11, 12) patts.

Between Stitch

row 2: 2 ch, * miss 2 htr, 2 htr in sp before next 2 htr, rep from *
ending 2 htr under 2 ch at beg previous row, turn. **
Rep this row 6 (8, 10) more times. 8 (10, 12) rows in all.

*** Shape Legs

inc row: 3 ch, 2 htr in 3rd ch from hook, patt as set ending 2 htr
under 2 ch, turn. 11 (12, 13) patts.
Rep this row 9 more times. 20 (21, 22) patts.
next row: 9 (11, 13) ch, 2 htr in 3rd ch from hook, [miss 1 ch, 2 htr
in next ch] 3 (4, 5) times, patt as set ending 2 htr under 2 ch, turn.
24 (26, 28) patts.
Rep this row once more. 28 (31, 34) patts.
Rep row 2 until straight part of work measures 11 (13, 15) cm
(4¼ [5, 6] in) from last row of leg shaping, ending WS row.
Fasten off.

HAT

round 1: using size 2.50 mm hook, make 5 ch and join into a ring with 1 ss in first ch made.

round 2: 2 ch, 11 htr into ring, 1 ss under 2 ch. 12 sts.

round 3: 2 ch, [2 htr in next htr] 11 times, htr in st at base of 2 ch, 1 ss in 2nd of 2 ch. 24 sts.

round 4: 2 ch, [1 htr in next htr, 2 htr in foll htr] 11 times, 1 htr in next htr, 1 htr in st at base of 2 ch, 1 ss in 2nd of 2 ch. 36 sts.

Check tension here: pull gently on starting end of yarn to tighten centre. First 4 rounds should measure 4 cm (1½ in) in diameter.

round 5: 2 ch, * [1 htr in next htr] twice, 2 htr in foll htr, rep from * 10 more times, [1 htr in next htr] twice, 1 htr in st at base of 2 ch, 1 ss in 2nd of 2 ch. 48 sts.

round 6: 2 ch, * [1 htr in next htr] 3 times, 2 htr in foll htr, rep from * 10 more times, [1 htr in next htr] 3 times, 1 htr in st at base of 2 ch, 1 ss in 2nd of 2 ch. 60 sts.

round 7: 2 ch, * [1 htr in next htr] 4 times, 2 htr in foll htr, rep from * 10 more times, [1 htr in next htr] 4 times, 1 htr in st at base of 2 ch, 1 ss in 2nd of 2 ch. 72 sts.

round 8: 2 ch, * [1 htr in next htr] 5 times, 2 htr in foll htr, rep from * 10 more times, [1 htr in next htr] 5 times, 1 htr in st at base of 2 ch, 1 ss in 2nd of 2 ch. 84 sts.

2nd size only

round 9: 2 ch, * [1 htr in next htr] 13 times, 2 htr in foll htr, rep from * 4 more times, [1 htr in next htr] 13 times, 1 htr in st at base of 2 ch, 1 ss in 2nd of 2 ch. 90 sts.

3rd size only

round 9: 2 ch, * [1 htr in next htr] 6 times, 2 htr in foll htr, rep from * 10 more times, [1 htr in next htr] 6 times, 1 htr in st at base of 2 ch, 1 ss in 2nd of 2 ch. 96 sts.

All Sizes

84 (90, 96) sts.

next round: 2 ch, 1 htr in each htr ending 1 ss in 2nd of 2 ch.
Rep this round until work measures 10.5 (12, 14) cm (4 [4¾, 5½] in) from centre to outside edge, ending with a complete round.

BRIM

brim round 1: 2 ch, [1 htr in each of 13 (14, 15) htr, 2 htr in next htr] 5 times, 1 htr in each of 13 (14, 15) htr, 1 htr in st at base of 2 ch, 1 ss in 2nd of 2 ch. 90 (96, 102) sts.

brim round 2: 2 ch, miss 2 htr, * 2 htr in sp before next htr, miss 2 htr, rep from * ending 1 htr in base of 2 ch, 1 ss in 2nd of 2 ch.

brim round 3: 2 ch, 1 htr in sp at base of these 2 ch, * miss 2 htr, 2 htr in sp before next htr, rep from * ending 1 ss in 2nd of 2 ch.
Rep brim rounds 2 and 3 until Brim measures 4 (4.5, 5) cm (1½ [1¾, 2] in) ending with a complete round.

next round: 1 ch, 1 dc in each htr ending 1 ss in 1 ch.

foll round: * 2 ch, 1 ss in st at base of these 2 ch (a picot made), 1 dc in each of next 2 dc, rep from * all round, ending 1 ss in base of 2 ch at beg of round. Fasten off.
Press as instructed on ball band.

FRONT

Work as Back to **.
Rep row 2, 2 (4, 6) more times. 4 (6, 8) rows in all.
Work as Back from *** to end.

WAISTBAND

Join side seams. Using shirring elastic double, make a ring to fit comfortably around waist, knotting securely and leaving ends at least 5 cm (2 in) long.
With RS of work facing, using size 2.50 mm hook, join yarn to top of one side seam.

round 1: 1 ch, * 1 dc over elastic ring and into next htr, rep from * ending 1 ss in 1 ch at beg of round. (Work over ends of knot at same time.)

round 2: * 2 ch, 1 ss in st at base of these 2 ch (a picot made), 1 dc in each of next 2 dc, rep from * all round, ending 1 ss in base of 2 ch at beg of round. Fasten off.

LEG AND CROTCH BORDER

With RS of work facing, using 2.00 mm hook, join yarn at base of one side seam.

round 1: 1 ch, *[1 dc in base of next ch, 2 dc tog over base of next 2 ch] 2 (3, 3) times, 1 dc in base of each of next 1 (0, 2) ch, 1 dc in side edge of each row to corner, 3 dc in same place at corner, 1 dc in base of each ch across crotch, 3 dc in same place at corner, 1 dc in side edge of each row, 1 dc in base of each of next 1 (0, 2) ch, [2 dc tog over base of next 2 ch, 1 dc in next ch] 2 (3, 3) times to side seam, rep from * once more ending 1 ss in 1 ch at beg of round.

round 2: * [2 ch, 1 ss in st at base of 2 ch, 1 dc in each of next 2 dc] to first corner, 3 dc in same place at corner, 1 dc in each dc across straight edge of crotch, 3 dc in same place at corner, rep from * once more, rep [ ] ending 1 ss in base of 2 ch at beg of round. Fasten off.

TO FINISH

Lap back crotch over front and sew on 3 poppers to fasten.
Press as instructed on ball bands.

JACKET, PANTS AND BOOTIES

WARM AS TOAST! A SNUG AND PRACTICAL OUTFIT, WITH EASY
POPPER FASTENING ON THE PANTS.

SIZES (see also page 20)

JACKET

to fit chest	36	41	46 cm
	14	16	18 in
actual measurement	40	46	52 cm
	15¾	18	20½ in
length to back neck	19	23	27.5 cm
	7½	9	11 in
sleeve seam with cuff	12	14	17.5 cm
folded back	4¾	5½	6¾ in

PANTS

to fit hips	41	46	51 cm
	16	18	20 in
actual measurement	51	55	59 cm
	20	21¾	23¼ in
length to front waist	30	33	36 cm
	12	13	14¼ in

BOOTIES

to fit foot length	8	9	10 cm
	3	3½	4 in

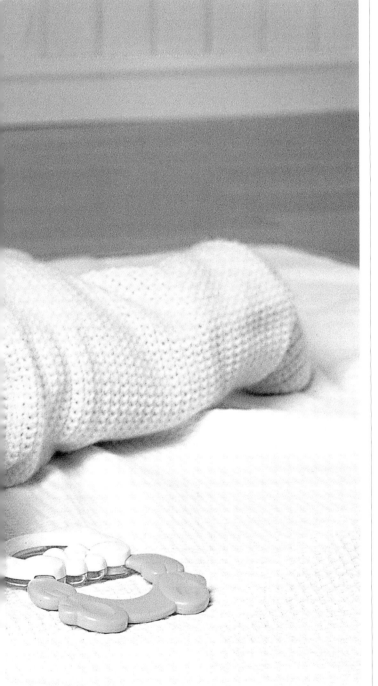

MATERIALS

JACKET
2 (2, 2) x 50 g balls of Sirdar Snuggly 4-ply in col.252 Lemon
5 (5, 6) buttons
3.50 mm and 3.00 mm hooks
PANTS
2 (2, 3) x 50 g balls of Sirdar Snuggly 4-ply in col.252 Lemon
shirring elastic
7 (7, 9) popper fasteners
3.50 mm and 3.00 mm hooks
BOOTIES
1 (1, 1) x 50 g ball of Sirdar Snuggly 4-ply in col.252 Lemon
3.50 mm and 3.00 mm hooks
(NOTE: for the whole set, only 4 (4, 5) 50 g balls will
be required)

TENSION

13 patterns and 17 rows to 10 cm (4 in) measured over
Cluster Stitch using size 3.50 mm hook.
19 sts and 23 rows to 10 cm (4 in) measured over rows of
dc using size 3.50 mm hook.

JACKET

BACK

Using size 3.50 mm hook make 55 (63, 71) ch.
foundation row: 1 dc in 3rd ch from hook, * 1 ch, miss 1 ch, 1 dc
in next ch, rep from * to end, turn.
Cluster Stitch
patt row: 2 ch, miss first dc, 2 dc tog over first 2 ch sps, * 1 ch,
2 dc tog over last ch sp used and next ch sp, rep from * ending 2 dc
tog over last 1 ch sp and 2 ch sp at beg previous row, 1 ch, 1 dc in
same 2 ch sp, turn. 26 (30, 34) patts. (Count each 2 dc tog as
1 patt.)
Rep this row until Back measures 8 (10, 12) cm (3¼ [4, 4¾] in)
ending WS row.

CLUSTER STITCH

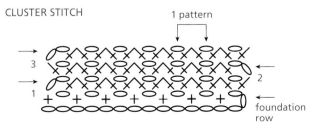

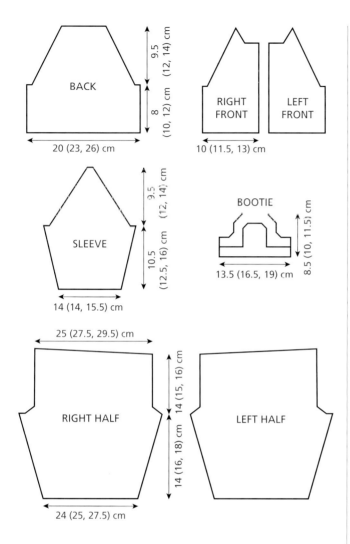

BACK

9.5 (12, 14) cm

8 (10, 12) cm

20 (23, 26) cm

RIGHT FRONT

LEFT FRONT

10 (11.5, 13) cm

SLEEVE

9.5 (12, 14) cm

10.5 (12.5, 16) cm

14 (14, 15.5) cm

BOOTIE

8.5 (10, 11.5) cm

13.5 (16.5, 19) cm

25 (27.5, 29.5) cm

RIGHT HALF

LEFT HALF

14 (15, 16) cm

14 (16, 18) cm

24 (25, 27.5) cm

Shape Raglan Armholes

dec row 1: ss across [1 ch, 2 dc tog] twice, 2 ch, patt until 22 (26, 30) patts are complete, 1 ch, 1 dc in next 2 dc tog, turn leaving [1 ch, 2 dc tog, 2 ch] unworked.

dec row 2: as patt row.

dec row 3: patt as set ending 2 dc tog over last 1 ch sp and 2 ch sp at beg previous row, turn.

dec row 4: 2 ch, miss 2 dc tog, patt as set ending 2 dc tog over last 1 ch sp and 2 ch sp at beg previous row, turn.

dec row 5: 2 ch, miss 2 dc tog, patt as set ending as end of patt row, turn. 20 (24, 28) patts.

2nd and 3rd Sizes Only

dec row 6: as patt row.

2nd Size Only

Rep dec rows 3–5 once.

3rd Size Only

Rep dec rows 3–6 once and 3–5 again.

All Sizes

20 (22, 24) patts.

Rep dec row 3 once.

Rep dec row 4, 9 times. 10 (12, 14) patts.

Rep dec row 5 once. Fasten off.

LEFT FRONT

Using size 3.50 mm hook make 29 (33, 37) ch.

Work foundation row and patt row as for Back. 13 (15, 17) patts.

Rep patt row until Back measures 8 (10, 12) cm (3¼ [4, 4¾] in) ending WS row. **

Shape Raglan Armhole

dec row 1: ss across [1 ch, 2 dc tog] twice, 2 ch, work 11 (13, 15) patts as set to end, turn.

dec row 2: as patt row.

dec row 3: as patt row.

dec row 4: patt as set ending 2 dc tog over last 1 ch sp and 2 ch sp at beg previous row, turn.

dec row 5: 2 ch, miss 2 dc tog, patt as set ending at end of patt row, turn. 10 (12, 14) patts.

2nd and 3rd Sizes Only

dec row 6: as patt row.

2nd Size Only

Rep dec rows 3–5 once.

3rd Size Only

Rep dec rows 3–6 once and 3–5 again.

All Sizes

10 (11, 12) patts.

Rep dec rows 4 and 5, 2 (2, 1) times.

Rep dec row 4 once more. 8 (9, 11) patts.

Shape Front Neck

1st row: 2 ch, miss 2 dc tog, 2 dc tog over first 2 ch sps, [1 ch, 2 dc tog over last ch sp used and next ch sp] 4 (4, 5) times, turn. 5 (5, 6) patts.

2nd row: 2 ch, miss 2 dc tog, patt as set ending 2 dc tog over last 2 ch sps, turn. 4 (4, 5) patts.

3rd and 4th rows: as 2nd row. 2 (2, 3) patts.

3rd Size Only

5th row: as dec row 5.

6th row: as dec row 4.

All Sizes

2 patts.

next row: 2 ch, 2 dc tog over first and last ch sps, 1 ch, 1 dc in last ch sp, turn.

foll row: 2 ch, 2 dc tog over first and last ch sps. 1 patt. Fasten off.

RIGHT FRONT

Work as Left Front to **.

Shape Raglan Armhole

dec row 1: 2 ch, patt until 11 (13, 15) patts are complete, 1 ch, 1 dc in next 2 dc tog, turn, leaving [1 ch sp, 2 dc tog, 2 ch] unworked.

dec row 2: as patt row.

dec row 3: patt as set ending 2 dc tog over last 2 ch sps, turn.

dec row 4: 2 ch, miss 2 dc tog, patt as set to end, turn.

dec rows 5 and 6: as patt row. 10 (12, 14) patts.

2nd and 3rd Sizes Only

Rep dec rows 3–6 (once, twice) more.

All Sizes

10 (11, 12) patts.

Rep dec rows 3 and 4, 2 (2, 1) times. 8 (9, 11) patts.

Shape Front Neck

1st row: ss across [1 ch, 2 dc tog] 3 (4, 5) times, 2 ch, 2 dc tog over next 2 ch sps, [1 ch, 2 dc tog over last ch sp used and next ch sp] 4 (4, 5) times, turn. 5 (5, 6) patts.

2nd row: 2 ch, miss 2 dc tog, patt as set ending 2 dc tog over last 2 ch sps, turn. 4 (4, 5) patts.

3rd row: as 2nd row.

4th row: as dec row 4. 2 (2, 3) patts.

3rd Size Only

5th row: as dec row 3.

6th row: as dec row 4.
All Sizes
2 patts.
next row: as dec row 3
foll row: 2 ch, miss 2 dc tog, 2 dc tog over first and last ch sps, 1 ch, 1 dc in last ch sp. 1 patt. Fasten off.

SLEEVES (make 2)
Using size 3.50 mm hook make 43 (43, 47) ch.
Work foundation row and patt row as for Back. 20 (20, 22) patts.
inc row 1: 2 ch, 2 dc tog over st at base of this ch and first ch sp, patt as set to end, turn.
inc row 2: as inc row 1. 22 (22, 24) patts.
inc rows 3 and 4: as patt row.
Rep these 4 rows 1 (2, 3) more times. 24 (26, 30) patts.
Rep inc rows 1 and 2 once more. 26 (28, 32) patts.
Rep patt row until Sleeve measures 10.5 (12.5, 16) cm (4¼ [5, 6¼] in) in all ending WS row.
Shape Raglan Sleeve
dec row 1: ss across [1 ch, 2 dc tog] twice, 2 ch, work in patt until 22 (24, 28) patts are complete, 1 ch, 1 dc in next 2 dc tog, turn leaving [1 ch, 2 dc tog, 2 ch] unworked.
dec row 2: as patt row.
dec row 3: patt as set ending 2 dc tog over last 1 ch sp and 2 ch sp at beg previous row, turn.
dec row 4: 2 ch, miss first 2 dc tog, patt as set ending 2 dc tog over last 1 ch sp and 2 ch sp at beg previous row, turn. 21 (23, 27) patts.

Rep dec row 4, 5 (11, 15) more times. 16 (12, 12) patts.
next row: 2 ch, miss first ch sp, 2 dc tog over next 2 ch sps, * 1 ch, 2 dc tog over last ch sp used and next ch sp, rep from * ending 2 dc tog over last 2 ch sps, turn. 14 (10, 10) patts.
Rep this row 6 (4, 4) more times. 2 patts. Fasten off.

TO FINISH
Join raglan seams. Join side and sleeve seams.
CUFFS (make 2)
With r. s. of work facing, using size 3.00 mm hook join yarn at base of sleeve seam.
round 1: 1 ch, 1 dc in base of each ch ending 1 dc in first dc of round.
round 2: 1 dc in each dc all round.
Rep round 2, 5 times, ending at underarm. Fasten off.
Fold cuff back.

FRONT, NECK AND LOWER BORDER

With RS of work facing using size 3.00 mm hook join yarn at base of one side seam.

round 1: 1 ch, 1 dc in each ch sp and base of each dc to corner, 3 dc in same place at corner, 1 dc in side edge of each row up right front edge, 3 dc in same place at corner, 42 (50, 58) dc evenly around neck to top of left front edge, 3 dc in same place at corner, 1 dc in side edge of each row down left front edge, 3 dc in same place at corner and 1 dc in each ch sp and base of each dc ending 1 ss in first dc of round.

round 2: 1 ch, 1 dc in first dc, 1 dc in each dc, working 3 dc in 2nd of 3 dc at each outer corner, ending miss last dc, 1 ss in first dc of round

to button left front over right: round 3: work as round 2 ending 3 dc in 2nd of 3 dc at top of left front edge, [2 ch, miss 2 dc, 1 dc in each of 4 (5, 5) dc] 4 (4, 5) times, 2 ch, miss next 2 dc, complete as round 2.

(to button right front over left: round 3: work as round 2 ending 3 dc in 2nd of 3 dc at bottom of right front edge, count down 27 (31, 38) dc from 2nd of 3 dc at next corner and place a marker on this st, 1 dc in each dc ending with marked st, [2 ch, miss 2 dc, 1 dc in each of 4 (5, 5) dc] 4 (4, 5) times, 2 ch, miss next 2 dc,

complete as round 2.)

both versions: round 4: 1 ch, 1 dc in first dc, 1 dc in each dc, 3 dc in 2nd of 3 dc at each corner and 2 dc in each 2 ch sp, ending miss last dc, 1 ss in first dc of round. Fasten off.

Sew on buttons to match buttonholes.

Press as instructed on ball bands.

PANTS

RIGHT HALF

Using size 3.50 mm hook make 47 (49, 53) ch.

foundation row: 1 dc in 2nd ch from hook, 1 dc in each ch to end, turn. 46 (48, 52) dc.

dc row: 1 ch, 1 dc in first dc, 1 dc in each dc to end, turn.

Shape Leg

inc row 1: 1 ch, 2 dc in first dc, 1 dc in each dc to end, turn.

inc row 2: as inc row 1.

inc rows 3 and 4: as dc row. 48 (50, 54) dc.

Rep these 4 rows 6 (7, 8) more times. 60 (64, 70) dc.

Rep dc row until work measures 14 (16, 18) cm (5½ [6¼, 7] in) ending WS row. * Place a marker at beg of last row.

Shape Top of Pants

1st row: ss across 4 dc, 1 ch, 2 dc tog over next 2 dc, 1 dc in each dc to last 2 dc, 2 dc tog, turn.

2nd row: 1 ch, 2 dc tog over first 2 sts, 1 dc in each dc to last 2 sts, 2 dc tog, turn.

Rep 2nd row 2 (2, 3) more times. 48 (52, 56) sts.

Rep dc row until work measures 28 (31, 34) cm (11 [12¼, 13¼] in) in all ending WS row.

Shape Waist

waist row 1: 1 ch, 1 dc in first dc, 1 dc in each of next 35 (38, 41) dc, 1 ss in next dc, turn.

waist row 2: 1 ch, miss 1 ss, 1 dc in each st to end, turn.

waist row 3: 1 ch, 1 dc in first dc, 1 dc in each of next 23 (25, 27) dc, 1 ss in next dc, turn.

waist row 4: as waist row 2.

waist row 5: 1 ch, 1 dc in first dc, 1 dc in each of next 11 (12, 13) dc, 1 ss in next dc, turn.

waist row 6: as waist row 2. Fasten off.

LEFT HALF

Work as Right Half to *.

Place a marker at end of last row.

Shape Top of Pants

1st row: 1 ch, 2 dc tog over first 2 dc, 1 dc in each dc to last 6 dc, 2 dc tog, turn.

2nd row: 1 ch, 2 dc tog over first 2 sts, 1 dc in each dc to last 2 sts, 2 dc tog, turn.

Rep 2nd row 2 (2, 3) more times. 48 (52, 56) sts.

Rep dc row until work measures 1 row less than Right Half at beg of waist shaping, ending RS row.

Shape Waist

Work waist rows 1–6 as for Right Half, without fastening off.

Work dc row once. Fasten off.

WAISTBAND

Join centre back seam and centre front seam down to markers.

Using shirring elastic double, make 2 rings to fit comfortably around waist, knotting each ring securely and leaving ends at least 5 cm (2 in) long.

With RS facing, using size 3.00 mm hook, join yarn at top of centre back seam.

round 1: 1 ch, * 1 dc over first elastic ring and into next dc, rep from * ending 1 ss in first dc of round. (Work over ends of knot at the same time.)

round 2: 1 ch, 1 dc in each dc ending 1 ss in first dc of round.

Rep round 2 once more.

Rep round 1 working over second elastic ring. Fasten off.

LEG AND ANKLE BORDER

With RS of work facing, using size 3.00 mm hook, join yarn at base of centre back seam.

round 1: 1 ch, * 1 dc in side edge of each row of leg to corner, 3 dc in same place at corner, work along ankle edge in base of ch: 1 dc in next dc, [2 dc tog over next 2 dc, 1 dc in next dc] 14 (15, 16) times, 1 dc in each dc to corner, 3 dc in same place at corner, 1 dc in side edge of each row to centre front seam, rep from * once more ending at centre back seam, 1 ss in first dc of round.

round 2: 1 ch, 1 dc in first dc, 1 dc in each dc and 3 dc in 2nd of 3 dc at each corner, ending miss last dc, 1 ss in first dc of round.

Rep round 2, 3 more times. Fasten off.

Lap front of border over back. Sew one popper to fasten at centre, one at each ankle and 2 (2, 3) more on each leg, evenly spaced. Press as instructed on ball bands.

BOOTIES (make 2)

Begin at ankle: using size 3.50 mm hook make 27 (32, 37) ch.

row 1 (WS row): 1 dc in 2nd ch from hook, 1 dc in each ch to end, turn. 26 (31, 36) dc.

dc row: 1 ch, 1 dc in first dc, 1 dc in each dc to end, turn.

Rep dc row 2 (2, 4) more times. 4 (4, 6) rows.

Shape Top of Foot

1st row (WS row): 1 ch, 1 dc in first dc, 1 dc in each of next 16 (19, 22) dc, turn.

2nd row: 1 ch, 1 dc in first dc, 1 dc in each of next 7 (8, 9) dc, turn. 8 (9, 10) dc.

Work 5 (7, 9) dc rows on these 8 (9, 10) sts.

next row: 1 ch, 2 dc tog over first 2 dc, 1 dc in each dc to last 2 dc, 2 dc tog, turn.

Rep this row once more. 4 (5, 6) sts. Fasten off.

Sides of Foot

With WS of work facing rejoin yarn at turn of 1st row of foot, 1 ch, 1 dc in each of 9 (11, 13) dc to end, turn.

foot row 1: 1 ch, 1 dc in each of 9 (11, 13) dc, work 9 (11, 13) dc up side edge of foot, 4 (5, 6) dc across toe, 9 (11, 13) dc down side edge of foot and 1 dc in each of 9 (11, 13) dc remaining from 2nd row. 40 (49, 58) dc, turn.

Work dc row 3 times.

dec row 1: 1 ch, 1 dc in first dc, 1 dc in each of 15 (19, 23) dc, 2 dc tog over next 2 dc, 1 dc in each of 4 (5, 6) dc, 2 dc tog over next 2 dc, 1 dc in each of 16 (20, 24) dc to end, turn. 38 (47, 56) dc.

dec row 2: 1 ch, 2 dc tog over first 2 dc, 1 dc in each st to last 2 dc, 2 dc tog, turn. 36 (45, 54) dc.

dec row 3: 1 ch, 1 dc in first st, 1 dc in each of 14 (18, 22) dc, 2 dc tog over next 2 dc, 1 dc in each of 2 (3, 4) dc, 2 dc tog over next 2 dc, 1 dc in each of 15 (19, 23) sts to end, turn. 34 (43, 52) dc.

dec row 4: as dec row 2. 32 (41, 50) dc.

2nd and 3rd Sizes Only

dec row 5: 1 ch, 1 dc in first st, 1 dc in each of (17, 21) dc, 2 dc tog over next 2 dc, 1 dc in each of (1, 2) dc, 2 dc tog over next 2 dc, 1 dc in each of (18, 22) sts to end, turn. (39, 48) dc.

3rd Size Only

dec row 6: as dec row 2.

All Sizes

32 (39, 46) sts. Fasten off.

Fold last row in half and join with a flat seam. Join side edges of rows to form heel seam.

Ankle Cuff

With RS of work facing, using size 3.00 mm hook, join yarn at top of heel seam.

round 1: 1 ch, 1 dc in base of each dc ending 1 dc in first dc of round.

round 2: 1 dc in each dc all round.

Rep round 2, 4 (5, 6) more times ending at centre back.

Change to size 3.50 mm hook and rep round 2, 4 (5, 6) more times ending at centre back. Fasten off.

LACY JACKET

COMFORTABLE TO WEAR, WITH A CIRCULAR YOKE AND NO SIDE
OR SHOULDER SEAMS.

SIZES (see also page 26)

to fit chest	36	41	46 cm
	14	16	18 in
actual measurement	44	49	53 cm
	17¼	19¼	21 in
length to shoulder	23	26	29 cm
	9	10¼	11½ in
sleeve seam	11.5	13.5	16.5 cm
	4½	5¼	6½ in

MATERIALS

2 (2, 2) x 50 g balls of Sirdar Snuggly 4-ply in
col.213 Angelica
5 (5, 6) buttons
3.50 mm and 3.00 mm hooks

TENSION
8½ patterns and 14 rows to 10 cm (4 in) measured over
Speedwell Stitch using size 3.50 mm hook.
19 sts and 23 rows to 10 cm (4 in) measured over rows of
dc using size 3.50 mm hook.

Special Abbreviation: 1 dble dec: 2 dc tog worked over
next and foll alt st as follows: insert hook in next st, yrh,
pull through a lp, miss 1 st, insert hook in next st, yrh, pull
through a lp, yrh, pull through 3 lps on hook.

BODY (made in one piece to armholes)

Using size 3.50 mm hook make 111 (123, 135) ch.

foundation row (WS row): [1 htr, 1 ch, 1 htr] in 4th ch from hook,
* miss 2 ch, [1 htr, 1 ch, 1 htr] in next ch, rep from * to last 2 ch,
miss 1 ch, 1 htr in next ch, turn. 36 (40, 44) patts.

Speedwell Stitch

pattern row: 2 ch, [1 htr, 1 ch, 1 htr] in each 1 ch sp, ending 1 htr
under 2 ch at beg previous row, turn.
Rep this row until Body measures 14 (16, 18) cm (5½ [6¼, 7] in)
ending wrong side row. Fasten off.

SPEEDWELL STITCH

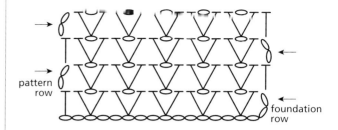

pattern row

foundation row

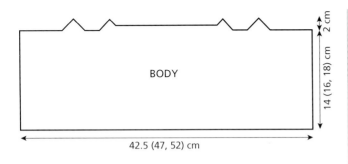

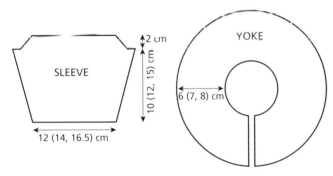

Shape Left Front

With right side of Body facing, leave first 3 (4, 5) patts, rejoin yarn to 1 ch sp at centre of next patt.

** dec row 1: 2 ch, * [1 htr, 1 ch, 1 htr] in next 1 ch sp, rep from * twice more, 1 htr in next 1 ch sp, turn.

dec row 2: 2 ch, 1 htr in first 1 ch sp, [1 htr, 1 ch, 1 htr] in next 1 ch sp, 2 htr tog over next 1 ch sp and 2nd of 2 ch at beg previous row, turn.

dec row 3: 2 ch, 2 htr tog over first 1 ch sp and 2nd of 2 ch at beg previous row. Fasten off. ******

Shape Back

With RS of Body facing, leave 2 whole patts along top edge after Left Front shaping, rejoin yarn to 1 ch sp at centre of next patt.

1st dec row: 2 ch, *[1 htr, 1 ch, 1 htr] in next 1 ch sp, rep from * 13 (15, 17) times, 1 htr in next 1 ch sp, turn.

2nd dec row: 2 ch, 1 htr in first 1 ch sp, * [1 htr, 1 ch, 1 htr] in next 1 ch sp, rep from * 11 (13, 15) times, 2 htr tog over next 1 ch sp and 2nd of 2 ch, turn.

First Side

dec row 3: 2 ch, 2 htr tog over first two 1 ch sps. Fasten off.

Second Side

With RS of Body facing, leave 8 (10, 12) whole patts along top edge of Body, rejoin yarn to centre of next patt, 2 ch, 2 htr tog over centre of next patt and 2nd of 2 ch. Fasten off.

Shape Right Front

With RS of Body facing, leave 2 whole patts along top edge after Back shaping, rejoin yarn to 1 ch sp at centre of next patt. Work as Left Front from ** to **.

SLEEVES (make 2)

Using size 3.50 mm hook make 33 (39, 45) ch.
Work foundation row and patt row as for Body. 10 (12, 14) patts.
Rep patt row 0 (1, 2) more times. 2 (3, 4) rows.

inc row 1: 3 ch, 1 htr in first htr, patt as set ending [1 htr, 1 ch, 1 htr] in 2nd of 2 ch at beg previous row, turn.

inc row 2: 3 ch, 1 htr in first 1 ch sp, patt as set ending [1 htr, 1 ch, 1 htr] under 3 ch at beg previous row, turn.

inc row 3: 2 ch, [1 htr, 1 ch, 1 htr] in first 1 ch sp and each 1 ch sp ending [1 htr, 1 ch, 1htr] under 3 ch at beg previous row, 1 htr in

2nd of these 3 ch, turn.

inc row 4: as patt row. 12 (14, 16) patts. 6 (7, 8) rows.
Rep inc rows 1–4, twice more. 16 (18, 20) patts. 14 (15, 16) rows.
Rep patt row until Sleeve measures 10 (12, 15) cm (4 [4¾, 6] in) in all ending WS row.

Shape Top of Sleeve

dec row 1: ss across [2 htr, 1 ch] twice, 2 ch, 12 (14, 16) patts as set, 1 htr in next 1 ch sp, turn.

dec row 2: 2 ch, 1 htr in first 1 ch sp, 10 (12, 14) patts as set, 2 htr tog over last 1 ch sp and 2nd of 2 ch, turn.

dec row 3: 2 ch, 1 htr in first 1 ch sp, 8 (10, 12) patts as set, 2 htr tog over last 1 ch sp and 2nd of 2 ch. Fasten off.

YOKE

Join sleeve seams. Join sleeves to body at each armhole, matching shaping rows.
With RS of work facing, using size 3.50 mm hook, join yarn at top of right front edge.

row 1: 1 ch, 16 (19, 22) dc along neck edge to seam, 29 (32, 35) dc across top of first sleeve, 30 (36, 42) dc across top of back, 29 (32, 35) dc across top of second sleeve, 16 (19, 22) dc along left front neck edge to end, turn. 120 (138, 156) dc.

row 2: 1 ch, 1 dc in first dc, 1 dc in each of next 3 (7, 9) dc, [2 dc tog over next 2 dc, 1 dc in each of next 8 (6, 5) dc] 11 (15, 19) times, 2 dc tog over next 2 dc, 1 dc in each of 4 (8, 11) dc to end, turn. 108 (122, 136) sts.

row 3: 1 ch, 1 dc in first dc, 1 dc in each st to end, turn.

row 4: as row 3.

row 5: 1 ch, 2 dc tog over first 2 dc, 1 dc in each of next 10 (8, 6) dc, [1 dble dec, 1 dc in each of next 6 (8, 10) dc] 9 times, 1 dble dec, 1 dc in each of next 10 (8, 6) dc, 2 dc tog over last 2 dc, turn. 86 (100, 114) sts.

rows 6–8: as row 3.

row 9: 1 ch, 2 dc tog over first 2 dc, 1 dc in each of next 8 (6, 4) dc, [1 dble dec, 1 dc in each of next 4 (6, 8) dc] 9 times, 1 dble dec, 1 dc in each of next 8 (6, 4) dc, 2 dc tog over last 2 dc, turn. 64 (78, 92) sts.

rows 10–12: as row 3.

row 13: 1 ch, 2 dc tog over first 2 dc, 1 dc in each of next 6 (4, 2) dc, [1 dble dec, 1 dc in each of next 2 (4, 6) dc] 9 times, 1 dble dec, 1 dc in each of next 6 (4, 2) dc, 2 dc tog over last 2 dc, turn. 42 (56, 70) sts.

row 14: as row 3.

1st Size Only

Fasten off.

2nd Size Only

row 15: 1 ch, 2 dc tog over first 2 dc, 1 dc in each of next 5 dc, [2 dc tog over next 2 dc, 1 dc in each of next 6 dc] 5 times, 2 dc tog over next 2 dc, 1 dc in each of next 5 dc, 2 dc tog over last 2 dc, turn. 48 sts.

row 16: as row 3. Fasten off.

3rd Size Only

row 15: 1 ch, 2 dc tog over first 2 dc, 1 dc in each of next 7 dc, [2 dc tog over next 2 dc, 1 dc in each of next 8 dc] 5 times, 2 dc tog over next 2 dc, 1 dc in each of next 7 dc, 2 dc tog over last 2 dc, turn. 62 sts.

row 16: as row 3.

row 17: 1 ch, 2 dc tog over first 2 dc, 1 dc in each of next 3 dc, [2 dc tog over next 2 dc, 1 dc in each of next 8 dc] 5 times, 2 dc tog over next 2 dc, 1 dc in each of next 3 dc, 2 dc tog over last 2 dc, turn. 54 sts.

row 18: as row 3. Fasten off.

TO FINISH
CUFF (make 2)
With RS of work facing, using size 3.00 mm hook join yarn at base of sleeve seam.

round 1: 1 ch, 1 dc in first ch sp, 2 dc in each ch sp ending 1 dc in last ch sp, 1 ss in first dc of round.

round 2: 1 ch, 1 dc in first dc, * 2 ch, 1 dc in each of next 2 dc, rep from * ending 1 ss in first dc of round. Fasten off.

FRONT, NECK AND LOWER BORDER
With RS of work facing using size 3.00 mm hook join yarn to one 2 ch sp on lower edge below one sleeve.

round 1: 1 ch, 1 dc in same ch sp, 2 dc in each ch sp ending 1 dc in last ch sp at corner, 3 dc in same place at corner, 42 (48, 54) dc evenly spaced up right front edge, 3 dc in same place at corner, 1 dc in each dc around neck to top of left front edge, 3 dc in same place at corner, 42 (48, 54) dc evenly spaced down left front edge, 3 dc in same place at corner and 2 dc in each ch sp along lower edge, ending 1 ss in first dc of round.

to button right front over left: round 2: 1 ch, 1 dc in first dc, 1 dc in each dc to corner, 3 dc in 2nd of 3 dc at corner, 1 dc in each of next 9 (15, 13) dc of Right Front edge, [2 ch, miss 2 dc, 1 dc in each of next 6 dc] 4 (4, 5) times, 2 ch, miss 2 dc, *1 dc in each dc to corner, 3 dc in same place at corner, rep from * all round ending 1 ss in first dc of round.

round 3: 1 ch, 1 dc in first dc, * 2 ch, 1 dc in each of next 2 dc, * rep * to * to corner, [2 ch, 2 dc] in 2nd of 3 dc at corner, 1 dc in each dc and 2 dc in each ch sp up Right Front edge to corner, [2 ch, 2 dc] in 2nd of 3 dc at corner, rep * to * along neck edge ending [2 ch, 2 dc] in 2nd of 3 dc at corner, 1 dc in each dc down Left Front edge to corner, [2 ch, 2 dc] in 2nd of 3 dc at corner, rep * to * along lower edge ending 1 ss in first dc of round. Fasten off.

(to button left front over right: round 2: work as round 2 above, but on right front edge work 1 dc in each dc, and on left front edge work 1 dc in first dc, rep [to] 4 (4, 5) times, 2 ch, miss 2 dc, complete as given.

round 3: work as round 3 above, working 1 dc in each dc on Front edges, and 2 dc in each 2 ch sp on Left Front edge. Fasten off.**)

Sew on buttons to match buttonholes.

Press as instructed on ball bands.

This delightful blue alternative has been crocheted in Sirdar Snuggly 4-ply in col.216 Sky.

TWO EASY JUMPERS

ONE BASIC PATTERN WITH A CHOICE OF TRIMS AND EDGINGS.

SIZES (see also page 30)

to fit chest	41	46	51 cm
	16	18	20 in
actual measurement	46	51	56 cm
	18	20	22 in
length to shoulder	25	28	30 cm
	9¾	11	11¾ in
sleeve seam	15	17	20 cm
	6	6¾	8 in

MATERIALS

LITTLE FLOWERS JUMPER
2 (3, 3) x 50 g balls of Wendy Peter Pan DK in col.A (300 Pure White)
small ball of Wendy Peter Pan DK in col.B (336 Delphinium)
4.00 mm and 3.50 mm hooks
4 buttons

STRAWBERRY JUMPER
2 (3, 3) x 50 g balls of Wendy Peter Pan DK in col.A (301 Spring Lamb)
small ball of Wendy Peter Pan DK in col.B (311 Miss Muffet)
oddment of Wendy Peter Pan DK in col.C (309 Leprechaun)
4.00 mm and 3.50 mm hooks
4 buttons

TENSION
16½ sts and 19 rows to 10 cm (4 in) measured over Double Crochet using size 4.00 mm hook.

DOUBLE CROCHET ROWS

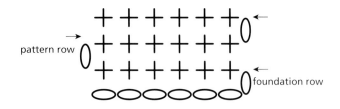

pattern row

foundation row

LITTLE FLOWERS JUMPER

BACK
Using size 4.00 mm hook and col.A make 39 (43, 47) ch.
foundation row: 1 dc in 2nd ch from hook, 1 dc in each ch to end, turn. 38 (42, 46) dc.
patt row: 1 ch, 1 dc in first dc, 1 dc in each dc to end, turn. *
Rep patt row until Back measures 22.5 (25.5, 27.5) cm (8¾ [10, 10¾] in) ending with a WS row.
Button Border: First Side
Change to size 3.50 mm hook.
1st row: 1 ch, 1 dc in first dc, 1 dc in each of next 10 (11, 12) dc, turn.
Work 3 more patt rows on these 11 (12, 13) sts. Fasten off.
Second Side
With RS of Back facing, leave 16 (18, 20) dc at centre back, using size 3.50 mm hook rejoin col.A to next dc.
1st row: 1 ch, 1 dc in same dc, 1 dc in each of 10 (11, 12) dc to end, turn.
Work 3 more rows of dc on these 11 (12, 13) sts. Fasten off.

FRONT
Work as given for Back to *.
Rep patt row until Front measures 8 (8, 10) rows less than Back to beg of Button Border, ending with a WS row.
Shape Front Neck: First Side
row 1: 1 ch, 1 dc in first dc, 1 dc in each of next 12 (13, 14) dc, 2 dc tog over next 2 dc, turn.
row 2: 1 ch, miss 2 dc tog, 1 dc in each of 13 (14, 15) dc, turn.
row 3: 1 ch, 1 dc in first dc, 1 dc in each of next 10 (11, 12) dc, 2 dc tog over next 2 dc, turn.
row 4: 1 ch, miss 2 dc tog, 1 dc in each of next 11 (12, 13) dc, turn.
Work a further 4 (4, 6) rows dc on these 11 (12, 13) sts.
Buttonhole Band
Change to size 3.50 mm hook.
Work 2 more rows.
buttonhole row: 1 ch, 1 dc in first dc, 1 dc in each of next 2 dc, 2 ch, miss 2 dc, 1 dc in each of next 3 (4, 5) dc, 2 ch, miss 2 dc, 1 dc in last dc, turn.
foll row: 1 ch, 1 dc in first dc, 1 dc in each dc and 2 dc in each 2 ch sp to end. Fasten off.
Second Side
With RS of Front facing, leave 8 (10, 12) sts at centre front, using size 4.00 mm hook rejoin col.A to next dc.
row 1: 1 ch, 1 dc in foll dc, 1 dc in each of 13 (14, 15) dc to end, turn.
row 2: 1 ch, 1 dc in first dc, 1 dc in each of 11 (12, 13) dc, 2 dc tog over last 2 dc, turn.

row 3: 1 ch, miss 2 dc tog, 1 dc in each of 12 (13, 14) dc to end, turn.

row 4: 1 ch, 1 dc in first dc, 1 dc in each of 9 (10, 11) dc, 2 dc tog over last 2 dc, turn.

row 5: 1 ch, 1 dc in 2 dc tog, 1 dc in each of 10 (11, 12) dc to end, turn.

Work a further 3 (3, 5) rows on these 11 (12, 13) sts.

Buttonhole Band

Change to size 3.50 mm hook.

Work 2 more rows.

buttonhole row: 1 ch, 1 dc in first dc, 2 ch, miss 2 dc, 1 dc in each of next 3 (4, 5) dc, 2 ch, miss 2 dc, 1 dc in each of next 3 dc to end, turn.

foll row: 1 ch, 1 dc in first dc, 1 dc in each dc and 2 dc in each 2 ch sp to end. Fasten off.

SLEEVES (make 2)

Lap buttonhole border over button border at each shoulder and stitch together at armhole edges. From base of each border count 22 (25, 28) rows down Back or Front and place a marker on side edge.

row 1: with RS of work facing, using size 4.00 mm hook and col.A work 37 (41, 45) dc evenly along armhole edge between markers, working through both thicknesses at shoulder (spacing is about 3 sts to every 4 rows), turn.

patt row: 1 ch, 1 dc in first dc, 1 dc in each dc to end, turn.

Rep patt row 0 (2, 4) more times. 2 (4, 6) rows in all.

dec row 1: 1 ch, miss first dc, 1 dc in each dc to end, turn.

dec row 2: as dec row 1.

dec rows 3 and 4: as pattern row. 35 (39, 43) sts. 6 (8, 10) rows in all.

Rep these 4 rows 4 (4, 5) more times. 27 (31, 33) sts. 22 (24, 30) rows in all.

Rep patt row until Sleeve measures 13.5 (15.5, 18.5) cm (5½ [6¼, 7½] in), or length required minus 1.5 cm (½ in). Fasten off.

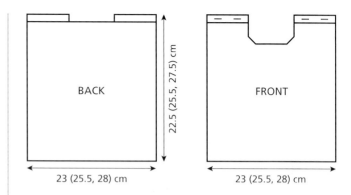

TO FINISH

Join side and sleeve seams by slip stitching on wrong side, matching row ends.

CUFF (make 2)

With right side of work facing, using size 3.50 mm hook and col.A, join yarn to 1 dc at sleeve seam.

SCALLOP BORDER

round 1: 1 ch, 1 dc in first dc, 1 dc in each dc, ending 1 dc under

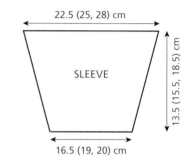

1 ch at beg of round. 27 (31, 33) dc.

round 2: 1 ch, 1 dc in first dc, 1 dc in each dc, working 2 dc tog 3 (3, 5) times evenly spaced, ending 1 ss in 1 dc at beg of round. 24 (28, 28) sts.

round 3: miss first dc, * 4 htr in next dc, miss 1 dc, 1 ss in next dc, miss 1 dc, rep from * ending 1 ss in last dc, 1 ss in first htr at beg of round. 6 (7, 7) patts. Fasten off.

LOWER BORDER

With right side of work facing, using size 3.50 mm hook and col.A, join yarn to base of 1 ch at one side seam.

round 1: as round 1 of Cuff. 76 (84, 92) dc.

round 2: 1 ch, 1 dc in first dc, 1 dc in each dc ending 1 ss in first dc of round.

round 3: as round 3 of Cuff. Fasten off.

BACK NECK BORDER

With right side of work facing, using size 3.50 mm hook and col.A, join yarn to corner of First Side Button Band.

row 1: 1 ch, work 19 (23, 25) dc evenly spaced along back neck edge, turn.

row 2: 1 ch, 1 dc in first dc, 1 dc in each dc, working 2 dc tog 2 (2, 4) times evenly spaced, turn. 17 (21, 21) dc.

row 3: miss first 2 dc, * 4 htr in next dc, miss next dc, 1 ss in next dc, miss next dc, rep from * ending 1 ss in last dc. 4 (5, 5) patts. Fasten off.

FRONT NECK BORDER

With right side of work facing, using size 3.50 mm hook and col.A, join yarn to corner of First Side Buttonhole Band.

row 1: 1 ch, work 32 (36, 40) dc evenly along neck edge,

row 2: 1 ch, 1 dc in first dc, 1 dc in each dc, working 2 dc tog 3 times evenly spaced, turn. 29 (33, 37) dc.

row 3: as row 3 of Back Neck Border. 7 (8, 9) patts. Fasten off. Sew on buttons to match buttonholes.

Press as instructed on ball bands.

FLOWER TRIM (make about 14)

round 1: using size 3.50 mm hook and col.B, make 5 ch and join into a ring with 1 ss in first ch made.

round 2: (work over starting end of yarn) 1 ch, 10 dc into ring, 1 ss in first dc of round.

round 3: * [1 htr, 1 tr, 1htr] in next dc, 1 ss in next dc, rep from * 4 more times. Fasten off, leaving yarn end about 25 cm (10 in). Pull gently on starting end of yarn to tighten centre. Arrange flowers on jumper following the photograph as a guide. Sew in place using long yarn ends. Press as instructed on ball bands.

FLOWER TRIM

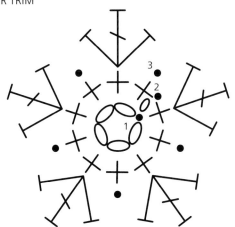

STRAWBERRY JUMPER

BACK, FRONT AND SLEEVES

Work in col.A as given for Little Flowers Jumper.

TO FINISH

Join side and sleeve seams by slip stitching on wrong side, matching row ends.

CUFF (make 2)

With right side of work facing, using size 3.50 mm hook and col.A, join yarn to 1 dc at sleeve seam.

LOOP BORDER

round 1: 1 ch, 1 dc in base of each dc, ending 1 dc under 1 ch at beg of round. 27 (31, 33) dc.

round 2: 1 ch, 1 dc in first dc, 1 dc in each dc, working 2 dc tog 5 times evenly spaced, ending 1 ss in 1 dc at beg of round. 22 (26, 28) sts.

round 3: 3 ch, miss 1 dc at base of these 3 ch, * 1 ss in next dc, 1 dc in next dc, 2 ch, rep from * ending 1 ss in first of 3 ch at beg of round. 11 (13, 14) patts. Fasten off.

LOWER BORDER

With right side of work facing, using size 3.50 mm hook and col.A, join yarn to base of 1 ch at one side seam.

round 1: as round 1 of Cuff. 76 (84, 92) dc.

round 2: 1 ch, 1 dc in first dc, 1 dc in each dc ending 1 ss in first dc of round.

round 3: as round 3 of Cuff. Fasten off.

BACK NECK BORDER

With right side of work facing, using size 3.50 mm hook and col.A, join yarn to corner of First Side Button Band.

row 1: 1 ch, work 19 (21, 23) dc evenly spaced along back neck edge, turn.

row 2: 1 ch, 1 dc in first dc, 1 dc in each dc, working 2 dc tog 3 times evenly spaced, turn. 16 (18, 20) dc.

STRAWBERRY MOTIF

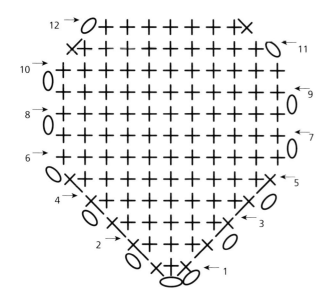

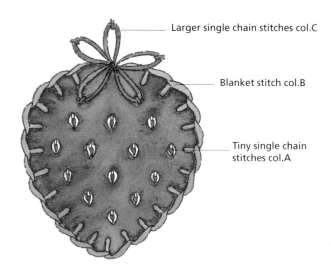

Larger single chain stitches col.C

Blanket stitch col.B

Tiny single chain stitches col.A

row 3: miss first dc, * 2 ch, 1 ss in next dc, 1 dc in next dc, rep from * ending 1 ss in last dc. 8 (9, 10) patts. Fasten off.

FRONT NECK BORDER
With right side of work facing, using size 3.50 mm hook and col.A, join yarn to corner of First Side Buttonhole Band.

row 1: 1 ch, work 32 (36, 40) dc evenly along neck edge, turn.

row 2: 1 ch, 1 dc in first dc, 1 dc in each dc, working 2 dc tog twice evenly spaced, turn. 30 (34, 38) dc.

row 3: as row 3 of Back Neck Border. 15 (17, 19) patts. Fasten off.
Sew on buttons to match buttonholes.
Press as instructed on ball bands.

STRAWBERRY MOTIF
Using size 3.50 mm hook and col.B make 2 ch.

row 1: 3 dc in 2nd ch from hook, turn.

row 2: 1 ch, 2 dc in first dc, 1 dc in next dc, 2 dc in last dc, turn. 5 dc.

row 3: 1 ch, 2 dc in first dc, 1 dc in each of 3 dc, 2 dc in last dc, turn. 7 dc.

row 4: 1 ch, 2 dc in first dc, 1 dc in each of 5 dc, 2 dc in last dc, turn. 9 dc.

row 5: 1 ch, 2 dc in first dc, 1 dc in each of 7 dc, 2 dc in last dc, turn. 11 dc.

row 6: 1 ch, 1 dc in first dc, 1 dc in each of 10 dc, turn.

rows 7, 8, 9 and 10: as row 6.

row 11: 1 ch, miss first dc, 1 dc in each of next 8 dc, 2 dc tog over last 2 dc, turn. 9 sts.

row 12: 1 ch, miss 2 dc tog, 1 dc in each of next 6 dc, 2 dc tog over last 2 dc. 7 sts. Fasten off.
Sew motif to centre front, about 5 cm (2 in) below neck edge, using col.B to work all round in blanket stitch as embroidery diagram. Use col.A to work tiny single chain stitches to represent seeds, and col.C to work larger chain stitches for leaves, as shown. See page 12 for diagrams of these embroidery stitches.
Press as instructed on ball bands.

STRIPED JUMPER AND RABBIT

SIMPLE TO MAKE AND EASY TO WEAR, WITH A POCKET THAT'S JUST THE RIGHT SIZE FOR A RABBIT.

SIZES

to fit chest	51	56	61 cm
	20	22	24 in
actual measurement	57.5	62.5	67.5 cm
	22½	24½	26½ in
length to shoulder	35.5	39.5	44 cm
	14	15½	17¼ in
sleeve seam	20.5	24	28 cm
	8	9½	11 in

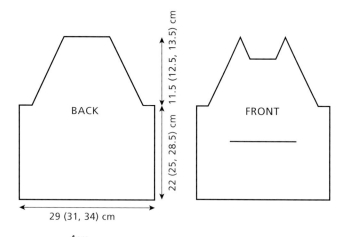

BACK

FRONT

11.5 (12.5, 13.5) cm

22 (25, 28.5) cm

29 (31, 34) cm

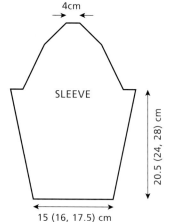

SLEEVE

4cm

20.5 (24, 28) cm

15 (16, 17.5) cm

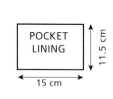

POCKET LINING

11.5 cm

15 cm

MATERIALS

2 (3, 3) x 50 g balls of Sirdar Calypso DK (double knitting cotton) in col.A (670 White)
2 (3, 3) x 50 g balls of Sirdar Calypso DK (double knitting cotton) in col.B (689 Azure Blue)
4.00 mm and 3.50 mm hooks
3 buttons

TENSION
16 sts and 17½ rows to 10 cm (4 in) measured over Stripe Pattern using size 4.00 mm hook.

Special Abbreviation: dcf: double crochet in front loop only of stitch below.

NOTE
When working in stripes, change colours as follows: at the end of 2nd and every alt row, work the last yrh and pull through in the colour required for the following row.

BACK

Using size 4.00 mm hook and col.A make 47 (51, 55) ch.
foundation row: 1 dc in 2nd ch from hook, 1 dc in each ch to end, turn. 46 (50, 54) dc.
next row: 1 ch, 1 dc in each dc to end, changing to col.B for last yrh, turn.
Stripe pattern
row 1: (using col.B) 1 ch, 1 dcf in each dc to end, turn.
row 2: 1 ch, 1 dc in each dcf to end, changing to col.A at end of row, turn.
row 3: (using col.A) as row 1.
row 4: as row 3, changing to col.B at end of row, turn.
These 4 rows form the Stripe Pattern. *
Rep them 8 (9, 11) more times.

STRIPE PATTERN

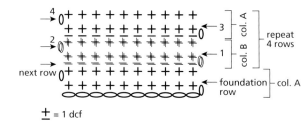

+ = 1 dcf

34

2nd size only
Work rows 1 and 2 once more.
All sizes
38 (44, 50) rows in all, ending 2 rows col.A (B, A).
Shape Raglan Armholes
** Continue throughout in Stripe Pattern as set:
1st dec row: ss across first 4 sts, 1 ch, 1 dcf in each dc to last 3 dc, turn, leaving last 3 sts unworked.
2nd dec row: 1 ch, 1 dc in each dcf, ending 1 dc in 1 ch at beg 1st dec row, turn. 40 (44, 48) sts.
3rd dec row: 1 ch, miss first dc, 1 dcf in each dc to end, leaving 1 ch at beg previous row unworked, turn.
4th dec row: 1 ch, miss first dcf, 1 dc in each dcf to end, leaving 1 ch at beg previous row unworked, turn. 38 (42, 46) sts. **
Rep 3rd and 4th dec rows 8 (9, 10) more times. 22 (24, 26) sts, ending 2 rows col.A.
Fasten off.

POCKET LINING
Using size 4.00 mm hook and col.A make 25 ch.
Work foundation row as for Back. 24 dc.
Work following row as for Back.
Rep Stripe Pattern rows 1–4 as for Back 4 times in all, and rows 1 and 2 once again. 20 rows in all, ending 2 rows col.B. Fasten off.

FRONT
Work as given for Back to *.
Rep the 4 Stripe Pattern rows 5 (6, 7) more times, and rows 1 and 2 once again. 28 (32, 36) rows, ending 2 rows col.B.
Place Pocket Lining
next row: (using col.A) 1 ch, 1 dcf in each of 11 (13, 15) dc, then work across top edge of Pocket Lining: with right side facing, 1 dcf in each of 24 dc; miss next 24 dc at centre of Front, 1 dcf in each of 11 (13, 15) dc to end, turn.
Work a further 9 (11, 13) rows Stripe Pattern. 38 (44, 50) rows in all, ending 2 rows col.A (B, A).
Shape Raglan Armholes
Work as given for Back from ** to **.
Rep 3rd and 4th dec rows 4 (5, 6) more times. 30 (32, 34) sts, ending 2 rows col.A.
Shape Front Neck: First Side
1st neck row: 1 ch, miss 1 dc, 1 dcf in each of next 8 dc, turn.
2nd neck row: 1 ch, miss 1 dcf, 1 dc in each dcf to end, turn.
3rd neck row: 1 ch, miss 1 dc, 1 dcf in each dc to end, turn.
Rep 2nd and 3rd rows twice more. 2 sts.
8th neck row: 1 ch, miss 1 dcf, 1 dc in last dcf. Fasten off.
Second Side
With right side of Front facing, leave 12 (14, 16) dc at centre front and rejoin col.B to next dc, 1 ch, 1 dcf in each of next 8 dc to end.
Work 2nd–8th neck rows as for First Side. Fasten off.

SLEEVES (make 2)
Using size 4.00 mm hook and col.A make 25 (27, 29) ch.
Work foundation row and following row as given for Back.
24 (26, 28) sts.
1st inc row: (using col.B), 1 ch, 2 dcf in first dc, 1 dcf in each dc to end, turn.
2nd inc row: 1 ch, 2 dc in first dcf, 1 dc in each dcf to end, turn.
3rd and 4th inc rows: (using col.A) work as Stripe Pattern.
26 (28, 30) sts.
Rep these 4 rows 6 (7, 8) more times. 38 (42, 46) sts.
30 (34, 38) rows in all.

Work a further 4 (6, 12) rows Stripe Pattern. 34 (40, 50) rows in all, ending 2 rows col.A (B, A).

Shape Raglan Sleeve

Work ** to ** as given for Back. 30 (34, 38) sts.

Rep 3rd and 4th rows 4 more times. 22 (26, 30) sts.

next dec row: 1 ch, miss first st, 1 dcf in each dc to last 2 sts, 2 dcf tog over last 2 sts, turn.

foll dec row: 1 ch, miss first st, 1 dc in each dcf to last 2 sts, 2 dc tog over last 2 sts, turn. 18 (22, 26) sts.

Rep these 2 rows 3 (4, 5) more times. 6 sts rem. Fasten off.

TO FINISH

Join raglan seams by slip stitching on wrong side, matching row ends, and leaving an opening of 12 rows (6 stripes) at top of Right Front raglan seam.

Join side and sleeve seams. Sew down Pocket Lining to wrong side of Front, matching stripes.

CUFF

With right side of work facing, using size 3.50 mm hook and col.B, join yarn to base of 1 ch at sleeve seam.

round 1: 1 ch, 1 dc in base of each ch, ending 1 dc under 1 ch at beg of round.

round 2: 3 ch, * 1 ss in each of next 2 dc, 2 ch, rep from * ending 1 ss in first of 3 ch at beg of round. Fasten off.

LOWER BORDER

With right side of work facing, using size 3.50 mm hook and col.B, join yarn to base of 1 ch at one side seam. Work rounds 1 and 2 as for Cuff. Fasten off.

NECK BORDER

With right side of work facing, using size 3.50 mm hook and col.B, join yarn to top of Right Sleeve.

row 1: 1 ch, 1 dc in each dc across top of Right Sleeve, back neck and top of Left Sleeve, 8 dc down side edge of front

neck shaping, 12 (14, 16) dc across centre front and 8 dc up side edge of front neck shaping, turn.

row 2: 1 ch, 1 dc in each dc to end, taking 2 dc tog at each of 4 corners of neck edge, turn.

row 3: 3 ch, * 1 ss in each of next 2 dc, 2 ch, rep from * ending 1 ss in last dc.

Do not fasten off but continue:

FRONT EDGE OF OPENING

row 1: 2 ch, 2 dc in side edge of neck border rows, 2 dc in side edge of each of 6 stripes, turn. 14 dc.

row 2: 1 ch, 1 dc in each of first 2 dc, [2 ch, miss 2 dc, 1 dc in each of next 3 dc] twice, 2 ch, miss 2 dc, 1 dc in 2nd of 2 ch, turn.

row 3: 1 ch, 1 dc in each dc and 2 dc in each ch sp to end.

Fasten off.

BACK EDGE OF OPENING

With right side of work facing, using size 3.50 mm hook and col.B, join yarn to side edge of first row at base of opening:

row 1: 1 ch, 1 dc in side edge of next row, 2 dc in side edge of each stripe, 2 dc in side edge of neck border rows, turn. 13 dc.

row 2: 1 ch, 1 dc in each dc to end. Fasten off.

Sew on buttons to match buttonholes.

Press as instructed on ball bands.

RABBIT TOY

SIZE

height   approx. 15 cm (6 in) excluding ears

MATERIALS

1 x 50 g ball of Sirdar Calypso DK (double knitting cotton) in col.A (676 Saffron)
4.00 mm hook
small amount of washable toy filling
oddment of black yarn, darning needle

TENSION
16 sts and 18 rows to 10 cm (4 in) measured over rows of dc using size 4.00 mm hook.

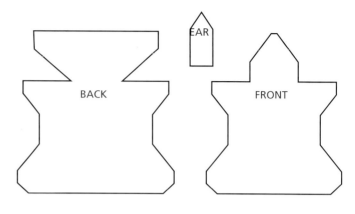

BACK
Using size 4.00 mm hook and col.A make 21 ch.
* **row 1:** 1 dc in 2nd ch from hook, 1 dc in each ch to end, turn. 20 dc.
row 2: 1 ch, 2 dc in first dc,1 dc in each dc to last dc, 2 dc in last dc, turn. 22 dc.
row 3: as row 2. 24 dc.
row 4: 1 ch, 1 dc in each dc to end, turn.
row 5: 1 ch, miss first dc, 1 dc in each dc to last 2 dc, 2 dc tog over last 2 dc, turn. 22 sts.
Rep this row, 4 more times. 14 sts.
Rep row 4, 3 more times. 12 rows in all.
row 13: as row 2. 16 dc.
Rep this row, 3 more times. 22 dc.
Work row 4 twice more. 18 rows in all. *
Shape head
row 19: 1 ss in each of first 8 dc, 1 ch, 1 dc in each of next 6 dc, turn.
row 20: 1 ch, 1 dc in each of 6 dc, turn.
row 21: 1 ch, 2 dc in first dc, 1 dc in next dc, [2 dc in next dc] twice, 1 dc in next dc, 2 dc in last dc, turn. 10 dc.
row 22: 1 ch, 2 dc in first dc, 1 dc in each of next 3 dc, [2 dc in next dc] twice, 1 dc in each of next 3 dc, 2 dc in last dc, turn. 14 dc.
row 23: 1 ch, 2 dc in first dc, 1 dc in each of next 5 dc, [2 dc in next dc] twice, 1 dc in each of next 5 dc, 2 dc in last dc, turn. 18 sts.
row 24: 1 ch, 2 dc in first dc, 1 dc in each dc to last dc, 2 dc in last dc, turn. 20 sts.
row 25: 1 ch, 1 dc in each of next 5 dc, 2 dc tog, 1 dc in each of next 6 dc, 2 dc tog, 1 dc in each of next 5 dc to end, turn. 18 sts.
row 26: 1 ch, 1 dc in each of next 4 dc, 2 dc tog, 1 dc in each of next 6 dc, 2 dc tog, 1 dc in each of next 4 dc to end, turn. 16 sts.
row 27: 1 ch, 1 dc in each of next 4 dc, 2 dc tog, 1 dc in each of next 4 dc, 2 dc tog, 1 dc in each of next 4 dc to end, turn. 14 sts.
row 28: 1 ch, 2 dc in first dc, 1 dc in each of next 2 dc, [2 dc tog] 4 times, 1 dc in each of next 2 dc, 2 dc in last dc, turn. 12 sts.
Fold top edge in half and work a row of ss through both edges together. Fasten off.

FRONT
Using size 4.00 mm hook and col.A, make 17 ch.
Work as given for Back from * to *. Note that there will be 4 sts less than given, throughout.
Shape Chin
row 19: 1 ss in each of first 6 dc, 1 ch, 1 dc in each of next 6 dc, turn.
row 20: 1 ch, 1 dc in each of 6 dc, turn.
Rep this row 3 more times.
row 24: 1 ch, 1 dc in each of next 2 dc, 2 dc tog, 1 dc in each of last 2 dc, turn. 5 sts.
row 25: 1 ch, 1 dc in each st to end, turn.
row 26: 1 ch, 1 dc in first dc, 3 dc tog, 1 dc in last dc, turn. 3 sts.
row 27: as row 25.
row 28: 1 ch, 3 dc tog. Fasten off.

EARS (make 2)
Using size 4.00 mm hook and col.A make 10 ch.
row 1: miss 3 ch, 1 tr in each of next 5 ch, 1 htr in next ch, [1 dc, 1 ch, 1 dc] in last ch, then continue along lower edge of ch: 1 htr between htr and next tr, [1 tr between next 2 tr] 4 times, 1 tr between last tr and 3 ch at beg of row 1. Fasten off leaving about 20 cm (8 in) end.

TO FINISH

Matching point of chin to end of seam at top of back head, join side edges, taking in slight fullness along top of each arm. Leave lower edge open. Insert toy filling and slip stitch lower edges together, spreading fullness evenly. Sew ears to top of head, gathering slightly to help them stand up.

Double the black yarn and thread the loop through the darning needle. At one side of head, in position for eye, pass needle under one stitch and through the loop of black yarn to secure. Then pass the needle through the head to the corresponding position on the opposite side and pull gently to shape the head. Make a small backstitch. For the eye, make a french knot in the same place, then pass the needle back through the head, pulling gently as before, make another backstitch and another french knot for the second eye. Run the needle inside the head through to the point of the nose and make about 4 straight stitches, fanned out from the point of the nose (see photograph). Secure with a backstitch and run the end inside the head.

ROSEBUD JUMPER

**QUICK TO MAKE IN DK YARN, WITH BORDERS
OF ROSEBUD MOTIFS.**

SIZES (see also page 42)

to fit chest	41	46	51 cm
	16	18	20 in
actual measurement	46	51	55 cm
	18	20	21¾ in
length to shoulder	24	27	29 cm
	9½	10½	11½ in
sleeve seam	15.5	17.5	20.5 cm
	6	6¾	8 in

BACK
Using size 4.50 mm hook make 40 (44, 48) ch.

Rosebud Border

row 1: (WS row) 1 tr in 3rd ch from hook, 1 tr in each ch to end, turn. 39 (43, 47) sts.

row 2: 2 ch, miss first tr, 1 tr in each of next 4 (2, 4) tr, * miss 2 tr, 3 tr tog in next tr, inserting hook behind this 3 tr tog, work 1 tr in each of 2 missed tr, 1 tr in same place as 3 tr tog, 1 tr in each of next 2 tr, inserting hook into same place as base of 3 tr tog work 3 tr tog, 1 tr in each of next 3 tr, rep from * ending 1 tr in each of 4 (2, 4) tr, 1 tr in 2nd of 2 ch, turn. 4 (5, 5) pairs of leaves.

ROSEBUD BORDER

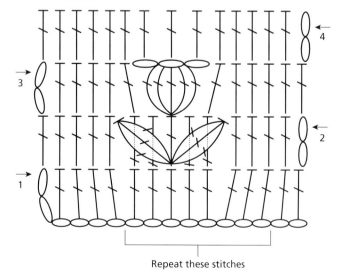

Repeat these stitches

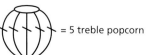 = 5 treble popcorn

MATERIALS

2 (3, 3) x 50 g balls of Wendy Peter Pan DK in
col.317 Candy Pink
4.50 mm and 4.00 mm hooks
4 buttons

TENSION

8½ patts and 17 rows to 10 cm (4 in) measured over Bud
Stitch using size 4.50 mm hook.

Special Abbreviation: 1 popcorn: (worked on WS row)
5 tr in next tr, remove hook from working loop, insert hook
through top of first of these 5 tr from back to front of
work, catch working loop and pull it through, thus
tightening top of popcorn and pushing it towards RS
of work.

row 3: 2 ch, miss first tr, 1 tr in each of 4 (2, 4) tr, * miss top of 3 tr tog, 1 tr in next tr, 1 ch, miss 1 tr, 1 popcorn in next tr, 1 ch, miss 1 tr, 1 tr in next tr, miss top of 3 tr tog, 1 tr in each of next 3 tr, rep from * ending 1 tr in each of 4 (2, 4) tr, 1 tr in 2nd of 2 ch, turn. 4 (5, 5) motifs.

row 4: 2 ch, miss first tr, 1 tr in each of 5 (3, 5) tr, * 1 tr in 1 ch sp, 1 tr in closing lp of popcorn, 1 tr in 1 ch sp, 1 tr in each of 5 tr, rep from * ending 1 tr in each of 5 (3, 5)tr, 1 tr in 2nd of 2 ch, turn. 39 (43, 47) sts.

Bud Stitch

preparation row: 1 ch, 1 dc in first tr, * miss 1 tr, 2 dc in next tr, rep from * ending 2 dc in 2nd of 2 ch, turn. 19½ (21½, 23½) patts.

patt row: 1 ch, 1 dc in first dc, * miss 1 dc, 2 dc in next dc, rep from * ending 2 dc in last dc. (Note that each pair of dc is worked in the second dc of pair as worked on previous row.) **
Rep patt row until Back measures 22 (25, 27) cm (8½ [9¾, 10½] in) ending WS row.

BUD STITCH

← pattern row

Button Border: First Side

Change to size 4.00 mm hook.

1st row: 1 ch, 1 dc in first dc, 1 dc in each of next 10 (12, 12) dc, 2 dc tog over next 2 dc, turn.

2nd row: 1 ch, miss 2 dc tog, 1 dc in each of 11 (13, 13) dc, turn.

3rd row: 1 ch, 1 dc in first dc, 1 dc in each dc to end. Fasten off.

Second Side

With RS of Back facing, leave 13 (13, 17) sts at centre back, using size 4.00 mm hook rejoin yarn to next dc.

1st row: 1 ch, 1 dc in each of next 12 (14, 14) dc to end, turn.

2nd row: 1 ch, 1 dc in first dc, 1 dc in each of 9 (11, 11) dc, 2 dc tog over last 2 dc, turn. 11 (13, 13) sts.

3rd row: 1 ch, 1 dc in first dc, 1 dc in each dc to end. Fasten off.

FRONT

Work as given for Back to **.
Rep patt row until Front measures 8 (8, 10) rows less than Back at beg of Button Border, ending with a WS row.

Shape Front Neck: First Side

1st neck row: 1 ch, 1 dc in first dc, [miss 1 dc, 2 dc in next dc] 7 (8, 8) times, turn. 15 (17, 17) sts.

2nd neck row: 1 ch, miss first dc, [miss 1 dc, 2 dc in next dc] 7 (8, 8] times, turn. 14 (16, 16) sts.

3rd neck row: 1 ch, 1 dc in first dc, [miss 1 dc, 2 dc in next dc] 6 (7, 7) times, turn. 13 (15, 15) sts.

4th neck row: 1 ch, miss first dc, [miss 1 dc, 2 dc in next dc] 6 (7, 7) times, turn. 12 (14, 14) sts.

5th neck row: 1 ch, 1 dc in first dc, [miss 1 dc, 2 dc in next dc] 5 (6, 6) times, turn. 11 (13, 13) sts.

Work a further 3 (3, 5) patt rows on these sts, thus ending length to match Back at beg of Button Border and with a WS row.

First Buttonhole Border

Change to size 4.00 mm hook.

1st row: 1 ch, 1 dc in first dc, 1 dc in each of next 10 (12, 12) dc, turn.

2nd row: 1 ch, 1 dc in first dc, 2 ch, miss 2 dc, 1 dc in each of next 3 (5, 5) dc, 2 ch, miss 2 dc, 1 dc in each of 3 dc to end, turn.

3rd row: 1 ch, 1 dc in each dc and 2 dc in each 2 ch sp to end. Fasten off.

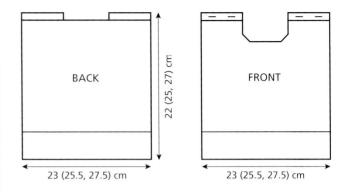

BACK

FRONT

22 (25, 27) cm

23 (25.5, 27.5) cm

23 (25.5, 27.5) cm

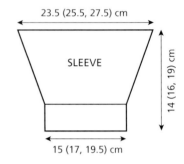

23.5 (25.5, 27.5) cm

SLEEVE

14 (16, 19) cm

15 (17, 19.5) cm

Second Side

With RS of Front facing, leave 9 (9, 13) sts at centre front, using size 4.50 mm hook rejoin yarn to next dc.

1st neck row: 1 ch, miss dc at base of this ch, [miss 1 dc, 2 dc in next dc] 7 (8, 8) times to end, turn. 14 (16, 16) sts.

2nd neck row: 1 ch, 1 dc in first dc, [miss 1 dc, 2 dc in next dc] 6 (7, 7) times, turn. 13 (15, 15) sts.

3rd neck row: 1 ch, miss first dc, [miss 1 dc, 2 dc in next dc] 6 (7, 7) times to end, turn. 12 (14, 14) sts.

4th neck row: 1 ch, 1 dc in first dc, [miss 1 dc, 2 dc in next dc] 5 (6, 6) times, turn. 11 (13, 13) sts.

Work a further 4 (4, 6) patt rows on these sts thus ending length to match First Side and with a WS row.

Second Buttonhole Border

Change to size 4.00 mm hook.

1st row: as 1st row of First Buttonhole Border.

2nd row: 1 ch, 1 dc in first dc, 1 dc in each of next 2 dc, 2 ch, miss 2 dc, 1 dc in each of 3 (5, 5) dc, 2 ch, miss 2 dc, 1 dc in last dc, turn.

3rd row: as 3rd row of First Buttonhole Border. Fasten off.

SLEEVES (make 2)

Using size 4.50 mm hook make 28 (32, 36) ch.

Rosebud Border

row 1: (WS row) 1 tr in 3rd ch from hook, 1 tr in each ch to end, turn. 27 (31, 35) sts.

row 2: 2 ch, miss first tr, 1 tr in each of next 2 (4, 2) tr, * miss 2 tr, 3 tr tog in next tr, inserting hook behind this 3 tr tog, work 1 tr in each of 2 missed tr, 1 tr in same place as 3 tr tog, 1 tr in each of next 2 tr, inserting hook into same place as base of 3 tr tog work 3 tr tog, 1 tr in each of next 3 tr, rep from * ending 1 tr in each of 2 (4, 2) tr, 1 tr in 2nd of 2 ch, turn. 3 (3, 4) pairs of leaves.

row 3: 2 ch, miss first tr, 1 tr in each of 2 (4, 2) tr, * miss top of 3 tr tog, 1 tr in next tr, 1 ch, miss 1 tr, 1 popcorn in next tr, 1 ch, miss 1 tr, 1 tr in next tr, miss top of 3 tr tog, 1 tr in each of next 3 tr, rep from * ending 1 tr in each of 2 (4, 2) tr, 1 tr in 2nd of 2 ch, turn.

3 (3, 4) motifs

row 4: 2 ch, miss first tr, 1 tr in each of 3 (5, 3) tr, * 1 tr in 1 ch sp, 1 tr in closing lp of popcorn, 1 tr in 1 ch sp, 1 tr in each of 5 tr, rep from * ending 1 tr in each of 3 (5, 3) tr, 1 tr in 2nd of 2 ch, turn. 27 (31, 35) sts. Rosebud Border complete.

inc row: 1 ch, 1 dc in first tr, [1 dc in each of next 6 (7, 8) tr, 2 dc in next tr] 3 times, 1 dc in each of 4 (5, 6) tr, 1 dc in 2nd of 2 ch, turn. 30 (34, 38) dc.

Bud Stitch

patt row: 1 ch, 1 dc in first dc, * miss 1 dc, 2 dc in next dc, rep from * ending 2 dc in last dc, turn. 31 (35, 39) dc.

Rep patt row 1 (3, 3) more times. 3 (5, 5) rows from last row of Rosebud Border, thus ending WS row.

inc row 1: 1 ch, 3 dc in first dc, * miss 1 dc, 2 dc in next dc, rep from * ending 2 dc in last dc, turn.

inc row 2: as inc row 1. 35 (39, 43) dc.

inc rows 3–6: as patt row.

Rep inc rows 1 and 2 once more. 39 (43, 47) dc.

Rep patt row until Sleeve measures 14 (16, 19) cm (5½ [6¼, 7½] in) or length required less 1.5 cm (⅝ in). Fasten off.

TO FINISH

Lap buttonhole border over button border at each shoulder and stitch together at armhole edges. On Back and Front, count 20 (22, 24) rows down from base of each border and place a marker on side edge.

Join top edges of sleeves to armhole edges between markers. Join side and sleeve seams, matching patts.

CUFF (make 2)

With right side of work facing, using size 4.00 mm hook join yarn to base of 1 ch at sleeve seam.

Picot Border

round 1: 1 ch, 1 dc in base of each ch, ending 1 dc under 1 ch at beg of round.

round 2: 1 ch, 1 dc in first dc, * 2 ch, 1 ss back in last dc

worked, 1 dc in each of next 2 dc, rep from * ending 1 ss in first dc of round. Fasten off.

LOWER BORDER

With right side of work facing, using size 4.00 mm hook, join yarn to base of 1 ch at one side seam.

Work 2 rounds of Picot Border as for Cuff.

BACK NECK BORDER

With right side of work facing, using size 4.00 mm hook, join yarn to corner of First Side Button Band.

row 1: 1 ch, work 20 (22, 24) dc evenly spaced along back neck edge, turn.

row 2: 1 ch, 1 dc in first dc, 1 dc in each dc, working 2 dc tog at each inner corner, turn. 18 (20, 22) dc.

row 3: 1 ch, 1 dc in first dc, * 2 ch, 1 ss back in last dc worked, 1 dc in each of next 2 dc, rep from * to end. 9 (10, 11) picots. Fasten off.

FRONT NECK BORDER

With right side of work facing, using size 4.00 mm hook, join yarn to corner of First Side Buttonhole Band.

row 1: 1 ch, work 30 (34, 38) dc evenly spaced along neck edge, turn.

row 2: 1 ch, 1 dc in first dc, 1 dc in each dc, working 2 dc tog 4 times evenly spaced, turn. 26 (30, 34) dc.

row 3: as row 3 of Back Neck Border. 13 (15, 17) picots. Fasten off.

Sew on buttons to match buttonholes.

Press as instructed on ball bands.

SLEEPING BAG

GENEROUSLY SIZED TO WEAR OVER NORMAL CLOTHES
(AND ALLOW FOR KICKING LEGS), THIS COSY SLEEPING BAG
IS IDEAL FOR TRAVELLING.

SIZES

to fit height	65–71	75–81 cm
	25¾–28	29½–32 in
to fit chest	41–46	51–56 cm
	16–18	20–22 in
actual measurement	65	75 cm
	25½	29½ in
length to shoulder	53.5	63 cm
	21	25 in
sleeve seam with cuff	15	18 cm
folded back	6	7 in

MATERIALS

6 (7) x 50 g balls of Patons Fairytale DK in col.A (6344 Lapis)
1 (1) x 50 g ball of Patons Fairytale DK in col.B (6300
Snow White)
3.50 mm and 4.00 mm hooks
12 (14) buttons

TENSION

16 trs and 8¾ rows to 10 cm (4 in) measured over rows of
trebles using size 4.00 mm hook.

TREBLE ROWS

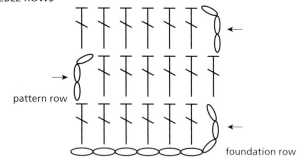

pattern row

foundation row

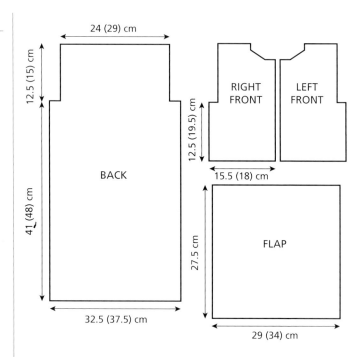

24 (29) cm

12.5 (15) cm

41 (48) cm

BACK

32.5 (37.5) cm

RIGHT
FRONT

LEFT
FRONT

12.5 (19.5) cm

15.5 (18) cm

27.5 cm

FLAP

29 (34) cm

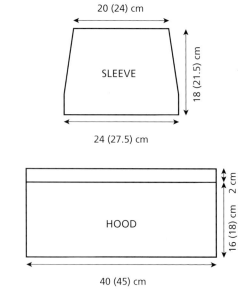

20 (24) cm

SLEEVE

18 (21.5) cm

24 (27.5) cm

2 cm

16 (18) cm

HOOD

40 (45) cm

BACK

Using size 4.00 mm hook and col.A make 54 (62) ch.

foundation row (RS row): 1 tr in 4th ch from hook, 1 tr in each ch to end, turn. 52 (60) sts. (First 3 ch count as first st.)

patt row: 3 ch, miss first tr, 1 tr in each tr ending 1 tr in 3rd of 3 ch at beg previous row, turn.

Rep patt row 34 (40) more times ending WS row. 36 (42) rows in all. Fasten off.

Shape Armholes

With RS of work facing, miss first 7 tr, rejoin yarn to next tr.

next row: 3 ch, 1 tr in foll tr, 1 tr in each of next 36 (44) tr, turn. 38 (46) sts.

Rep patt row 10 (12) times ending RS row. 47 (55) rows in all. Fasten off.

FLAP

With RS of Back facing, using size 4.00 mm hook and col.A join yarn to lower edge: miss base of first 3 tr, join yarn to base of next tr.

row 1: 3 ch, 1 tr in base of each of next 45 (53) tr, turn. 46 (54) sts. Rep patt row as for Back 5 times.

MOON MOTIF

Use Intarsia method (as page 13).

1st row: using col.A, 3 ch, miss first tr, 1 tr in each of next 6 (9) tr, work 26 trs from row 1 of chart (reading right to left) in cols as shown, using col.A work 1 tr in each of next 12 (17) tr, 1 tr in 3rd of 3 ch, turn.

2nd row: using col.A, 3 ch, miss first tr, 1 tr in each of next 12 (17) tr, work 26 trs from row 2 of chart (reading left to right) in cols as shown, using col.A work 1 tr in each of next 6 (9) tr, 1 tr in 3rd of 3 ch, turn.

Continue in this way reading from successive chart rows until chart row 14 is complete. 20 rows in all.

Continue in col.A: rep patt row 4 more times. 24 rows in all. Fasten off.

MOON MOTIF

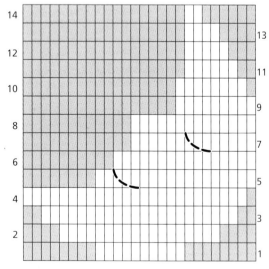

☐ col.A

▨ col.B

～ chain stitch using col.A

LEFT FRONT

Using size 4.00 mm hook and col.A make 27 (31) ch.

Work foundation row and row 1 as for Back. 25 (29) sts. Count foundation row as a WS row:

Rep patt row 9 (15) times ending with a WS row. 11 (17) rows in all.
**

Fasten off.

Shape Armhole

With RS of work facing, miss first 7 tr, rejoin yarn to next tr.

next row: 3 ch, 1 tr in next tr, 1 tr in each tr ending 1 tr in 3rd of 3 ch, turn. 18 (22) sts.

Rep patt row 5 (7) times ending WS row.

Shape Neck

1st row: 3 ch, miss first tr, 1 tr in each of next 13 (15) tr, 2 tr tog over next 2 tr, turn.

2nd row: 2 ch, miss 2 tr tog, 1 tr in each tr ending 1 tr in 3rd of 3 ch, turn.

3rd row: 3 ch, miss first tr, 1 tr in each of next 11 (13) tr, 2 tr tog over last 2 tr, turn.

4th row: as 2nd row. 12 (14) sts.

Rep patt row once more. Fasten off.

RIGHT FRONT

Work as given for Left Front to **.

Shape Armhole

next row: 3 ch, 1 tr in first tr, 1 tr in each of next 16 (20) tr, turn. 18 (22) sts.

Rep patt row 5 (7) times ending WS row. Fasten off.

Shape Neck

With RS of work facing, miss first 2 (4) tr, rejoin yarn to next tr.

1st row: 2 ch, 1 tr in each of foll 14 (16) tr, 1 tr in 3rd of 3 ch, turn.

2nd row: 3 ch, miss first tr, 1 tr in each of next 12 (14) tr, 2 tr tog over last 2 tr, turn.

3rd row: 2 ch, miss 2 tr tog, 1 tr in each tr ending 1 tr in 3rd of 3 ch, turn.

4th row: 3 ch, miss first tr, 1 tr in each of next 10 (12) tr, 2 tr tog over last 2 tr, turn. 12 (14) sts.

Rep patt row once more. Fasten off.

SLEEVES (make 2)

Join shoulder seams. Begin at shoulder edge:

With right side of work facing, using size 4.00 mm hook and col.A, join yarn at inner corner of armhole, 3 ch, 38 (44) tr evenly spaced along armhole edge, turn.

Rep patt row 3 (5) times. 4 (6) rows in all.

Shape Sleeve

dec row 1: 2 ch, miss first tr, 1 tr in each tr ending 1 tr in 3rd of 3 ch, turn.

dec row 2: 2 ch, miss first tr, 1 tr in each tr to last tr, miss top of 2 ch, turn.

dec row 3: 3 ch, miss first tr, 1 tr in each tr to last tr, miss top of 2 ch, turn.

dec row 4: 3 ch, miss first tr, 1 tr in each tr ending 1 tr in 3rd of 3 ch, turn. 36 (42) sts.

Rep these 4 rows, twice more. 32 (38) sts. 16 (18) rows in all.

Second Size Only

Rep patt row once more.

Both Sizes

16 (19) rows in all. Fasten off.

CUFF

Join sleeve seams, with first 4 rows worked matching armhole shapings.

Using size 3.50 mm hook and col.A, join yarn at base of sleeve seam.

round 1: 1 ch, 1 dc in first tr, 1 dc in each tr ending 1 ss in first dc of round.

round 2: 1 dc in each dc of round, working [2 dc tog over 2 dc] 4 times, evenly spaced.

round 3: 1 dc in each dc.

Rep round 3, 5 more times ending at sleeve seam with 1 ss in first dc of last round. 8 rounds in all. Fasten off.

HOOD

Using size 4.00 mm hook and col.A make 66 (74) ch.
Work foundation row and patt row as for Back. 64 (72) sts.
Rep patt row 12 (14) times. 14 (16) rows in all.

BORDER

Change to size 3.50 mm hook.

dec row: 1 ch, 1 dc in first tr, 1 dc in each of next 2 (3) tr, [2 dc tog over next 2 tr, 1 dc in each of next 6 (7) tr] 7 times, 2 dc tog over next 2 tr, 1 dc in each of last 2 tr, 1 dc in 3rd of 3 ch, turn. 56 (64) sts.

next row: 1 ch, 1 dc in first dc, 1 dc in each dc to end, turn.
Rep this row twice more. Fasten off.
Fold lower edge of hood in half and join to form centre back seam. Sew side edges to neck edge, gathering evenly along front neck edges.

FRONT BANDS

Join side seams, matching row ends beneath armholes.

to button left front over right:
Right Front Band
With RS of work facing, using size 3.50 mm hook, join col.A at lower corner of Back.

1st row: 1 ch, 2 dc in side edge of each row to corner, 3 dc tog at corner, 1 dc in base of each tr along lower edge of Right Front, 3 dc in same place at corner, 2 dc in side edge of each row up to beg of neck shaping, turn.

2nd row: 1 ch, 1 dc in first dc, 1 dc in each dc, working 3 dc in 2nd of 3 dc at outer corner and 3 dc tog at inner corner, to end, turn.

3rd and 4th rows: as 2nd row. Fasten off.

Left Front Band
Mark positions for 4 buttons on Right Front edge as follows: top one 2 sts down from neck edge, 1 at corner of Right Front and 2 more evenly spaced between.
With RS of work facing, using size 3.50 mm hook, join col.A at top of Left Front edge.

1st row: 1 ch, 2 dc in side edge of each row to corner, 3 dc in same place at corner, 1 dc in base of each tr along lower edge of Left Front, 3 dc tog at corner, 2 dc in side edge of each row down to lower corner of Back, turn.

2nd row: 1 ch, 1 dc in first dc, 1 dc in each dc, working 3 dc in 2nd of 3 dc at outer corner and 3 dc tog at inner corner, to end, turn.
Mark positions for 4 buttonholes to match positions for buttons on Right Front edge.

3rd row: as 2nd row, making a buttonhole to match each marker as follows: [2 ch, miss 2 dc].

4th row: as 2nd row, working 2 dc in each 2 ch sp. Fasten off.

(to button right front over left:
Work Left Front Band as above, omitting buttonholes, and mark positions for 4 buttons as given. Work Right Front Band as above, making buttonholes to match markers as given.**)**
At each lower corner of Back fold band in towards centre front and sew side edge of band to base of 3 tr at each side of Flap.

FLAP BORDER

With RS of work facing, using size 3.50 mm hook, join col.A at lower right corner of Flap.

1st row: 1 ch, 2 dc in side edge of each row to corner, 3 dc in same place at corner, 1 dc in each tr across top of Flap, 3 dc in same place at corner, 2 dc in side edge of each row to lower left corner, turn.

2nd row: 1 ch, 1 dc in first dc, 1 dc in each dc and 3 dc in 2nd of 3 dc at each corner, to end, turn.
Mark positions for 9 (11) buttonholes as follows: 1 at centre top to match lowest button on front edge, 1 at each corner of Flap, 2 more on top edge, evenly spaced between; 2 (3) on each side of Flap, evenly spaced.

3rd row: as 2nd row, making a buttonhole to match each marker as follows: [2 ch, miss 2 dc].

4th row: as 2nd row, working 2 dc in each 2 ch sp. Fasten off.
At each lower corner, sew down side edge of border.
Sew on buttons to match buttonholes.

STAR (make 3)

Using size 3.50 mm hook and col.B make 5 ch and join into a ring with 1 ss in first ch made.

round 1: * 3 ch, 1 dc in 2nd ch from hook, 1 htr in next ch, 1 ss in next ch of ring, rep from * 4 more times ending with last ss in base of first point of star. Fasten off.
Arrange the stars on the Flap following the photograph as a guide and stitch in place.
Using col.A, embroider mouth and eye on moon in chain stitch as indicated on chart.
Press as instructed on ball bands.

LACY CARDIGAN

COOL AND PRETTY IN SMOOTH COTTON YARN.

SIZES

to fit chest	51	56	61 cm
	20	22	24 in
actual measurement	59	63	67 cm
	23¼	24¾	26½ in
length to shoulder	27	32	37 cm
	10½	12½	14½ in
sleeve seam	20	25	29 cm
	8	9¾	11½ in

MATERIALS

6 (7, 9) x 25 g balls of Twilley's Lyscordet (3-ply cotton) in col.A (21 Ecru)

2.50 mm and 2.00 mm hooks

4 (5, 6) small buttons

TENSION

9½ patts and 17 rows to 10 cm (4 in) measured over Lacy Pattern using size 2.50 mm hook.

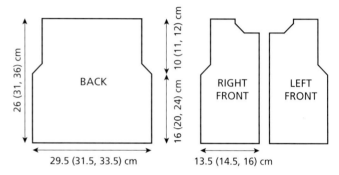

BACK

Using size 2.50 mm hook make 86 (92, 98) ch.

foundation row: 1 htr in 3rd ch from hook, * 1 ch, 1 htr in next ch, miss 1 ch, 1 htr in next ch, rep from * ending 1 htr in last ch, turn. 28 (30, 32) patts.

Lacy Pattern

pattern row: 2 ch, * miss 2 htr, [1 htr, 1 ch, 1 htr] in next ch sp, rep from * ending miss last htr, 1 htr in 2nd of 2 ch, turn.

Rep pattern row until Back measures 16 (20, 24) cm (6¼ [8, 9½] in) ending WS row.

LACY PATTERN

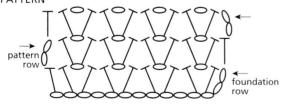

pattern row

foundation row

Shape Armholes

Place a marker at each end of last row.

dec row 1: 2 ch, 1 htr in first ch sp, patt as set ending 2 htr tog over last ch sp and 2nd of 2 ch, turn. 26 (28, 30) patts.

dec row 2: 2 ch [1 htr, 1 ch, 1 htr] in each ch sp, ending 1 htr in last htr, turn.

Rep these 2 rows, 3 more times. 20 (22, 24) patts.

Rep patt row until Back measures 26 (31, 36) cm (10¼ [12¼, 14] in) in all ending WS row. Fasten off.

LEFT FRONT

Using size 2.50 mm hook make 41 (44, 47) ch.

Work foundation row and patt row as for Back. 13 (14, 15) patts.

Rep patt row until length matches Back to beg armhole shaping ending WS row. **

Shape Armhole

Place a marker at end of last row.

dec row 1: 2 ch, 1 htr in first ch sp, patt as set to end. 12 (13, 14) patts.

dec row 2: patt as set ending 1 htr in last htr, turn.

Rep these 2 rows, 3 more times. 9 (10, 11) patts.

Rep patt row until length measures 8 (8, 10) rows less than Back ending WS row.

Shape Front Neck

1st row: 2 ch, 7 (7, 8) patts as set, 1 htr in next ch sp, turn.

2nd row: as patt row.

3rd row: patt as set to last ch sp, 1 htr in last ch sp, turn.

4th row: as patt row.

Rep 3rd and 4th rows once more. 5 (5, 6) patts.

Rep patt row 2 (2, 4) more times. Length matches Back. Fasten off.

RIGHT FRONT

Work as given for Left Front to **.

Shape Armhole

Place a marker at beg of last row.

dec row 1: patt as set to last ch sp, 2 htr tog over last ch sp and 2nd of 2 ch, turn. 12 (13, 14) patts.

dec row 2: 2 ch [1htr, 1ch, 1htr] in each ch sp ending 1 htr in 2nd of 2 ch, turn.

Rep these 2 rows, 3 more times. 9 (10, 11) patts.

Rep patt row until length measures 8 (8, 10) rows less than Back ending WS row. Fasten off.

Shape Front Neck

Rejoin yarn to 2nd (3rd, 3rd) ch sp of last row.

1st row: 2 ch, 7 (7, 8) patts as set to end, turn.

2nd row: as patt row.

3rd row: 1 ss in first ch sp, 2 ch, patt as set to end, turn.

4th row: as patt row.

Rep 3rd and 4th rows once more. 5 (5, 6) patts.

Rep patt row 2 (2, 4) more times. Length matches Back. Fasten off.

SLEEVES (make 2)

Using size 2.50 mm hook make 44 (50, 56) ch.

Work foundation row and patt row as for Back. 14 (16, 18) patts.

Rep patt row 2 (4, 4) more times. 4 (6, 6) rows.

inc row 1: 3 ch, 1 htr in st at base of these 3 ch, patt as set ending [1 htr, 1 ch, 1 htr] in 2nd of 2 ch, turn.

inc row 2: 3 ch, 1 htr in first ch sp, patt as set ending [1 htr, 1 ch, 1 htr] in 3 ch sp, turn.

inc rows 3 (3–4, 3–5): as inc row 2.

inc row 4 (5, 6): 2 ch, [1 htr, 1 ch, 1 htr] in first ch sp, patt as set ending [1 htr, 1 ch, 1htr] in last ch sp, 1 htr in 2nd of 3 ch, turn. 16 (18, 20) patts.

inc rows 5–6 (6–8, 7–10): as patt row. 10 (14, 16) rows in all.

Rep inc rows 1–6 (1–8, 1–10), twice more. 20 (22, 24) patts. 22 (30, 36) rows.

Work inc rows 1–4 (1–5, 1–6) once again. 22 (24, 26) patts.

Rep patt row until Sleeve measures 19 (24, 28) cm (7½ [9½, 11] in) in all.

Shape Top of Sleeve

Place a marker at each end of last row.

dec row 1: 2 ch, 1 htr in first ch sp, patt as set ending 2 htr tog over last ch sp and 2nd of 2 ch, turn. 20 (22, 24) patts.

dec row 2: as patt row.

Rep these 2 rows, 3 more times. 14 (16, 18) patts. Fasten off.

TO FINISH

Join shoulder seams. Join top edges of sleeves to armhole edges, matching shaping rows above markers. Join side and sleeve seams by slip stitching on wrong side, matching row ends.

COLLAR

With right side of work facing, using size 2.00 mm hook, join yarn to neck edge at top of Right Front.

row 1: work around neck edge: 1 ch, 1 dc in each htr and ch sp and 3 dc in side edge of each 2 rows, with 3 dc tog at each corner of back neck, along to top of Left Front edge, turn.

row 2: 1 ch, 1 dc in first dc, 1 dc in each st to end, turn.

Rep row 2 twice more.

row 5: as row 2, working 2 dc tog, one or more times, evenly spaced to make 51 (57, 63) sts, turn.

row 6: 2 ch, miss first dc, * [1 htr, 1 ch, 1 htr] in next dc, miss 1 dc, rep from * ending [1 htr, 1 ch, 1 htr] in next dc, 1 htr in last dc, turn.

row 7: 2 ch, * miss 2 htr, [1 htr, 1 ch, 1 htr] in next ch sp, rep from * ending miss last htr, 1 htr in 2nd of 2 ch, turn. 25 (28, 31) patts.

Rep row 7, 4 (6, 8) more times. Fasten off.

CUFF (make 2)

With right side of work facing, using size 2.00 mm hook, join yarn to base of sleeve seam.

Shell Border

round 1: 1 ch, * 1 dc in next ch sp, 2 dc tog over base of next 2 htr, 1 dc in next ch sp, 1 dc in base of each of next 2 htr, rep from * ending 1 ss in 1 ch at beg of round.

round 2: 1 ch, miss 1 dc, * [1 dc, 1 htr, 1 dc] in next dc, 1 ss in next dc, miss 1 dc, rep from *, ending 1 ss in 1 ch at beg of round. Fasten off.

Note: It may be necessary to adjust sts on round 2 to make a complete number of shells: miss an extra dc before 1 ss, one or more times, as required.

FRONT AND LOWER EDGE BORDER

With RS of work facing, using size 2.00 mm hook join yarn at left front base of collar.

row 1: 1 ch, work 3 dc in side edge of every 4 rows down front edge, 3 dc in same place at corner, work along lower edge in same way as for first round of Cuff, 3 dc at next corner, work up right front edge in same way as for left front edge to base of collar, turn.

buttonhole band: 1 ch, 1 dc in first dc, * 2 ch, miss 2 dc, 1 dc in each of next 10 dc, rep from * 2 (3, 4) more times, 2 ch, miss 2 dc, 1 dc in each dc to 2nd of 3 dc at first corner, turn and work back: 1 ch, 1 dc in each dc and 2 dc in each ch sp to end, turn. 4 (5, 6) buttonholes.

row 2: 1 ch, 1 dc in each dc to corner, 3 dc in same place, 1 dc in side edge of each row of buttonhole band, 1 dc in each dc along lower edge, 3 dc in 2nd of 3 dc at corner, 1 dc in each dc to end, turn.

button band: 1 ch, 1 dc in each dc to 2nd of 3 dc at first corner, turn and work back: 1 ch, 1 dc in each dc to end, turn.

shell row: 1 ch, miss first dc, * [1 dc, 1 htr, 1 dc] in next dc, 1 ss in next dc, miss 1 dc, rep from * ending 1 ss in last dc at top of right front edge. Fasten off.

Note: it may be necessary to adjust sts in same way as for Cuff to make the same number of shells on each front edge.

COLLAR BORDER

With underneath of Collar facing using size 2.00 mm hook join yarn at top corner of buttonhole band.

row 1: 1 ch, 3 dc across top of band, 3 dc tog at corner, 1 dc in side edge of each dc row, 3 dc in side edge of every 4 patt rows to corner, 3 dc in same place at corner, 1 dc in each htr and ch sp across top of collar, 3 dc in same place at corner, work down second side of collar in same way as first side, 3 dc tog at corner, 3 dc across top of band, 1 ss in first st of shell at corner, turn.

shell row: (adjusting sts if necessary as before) 1 ch, 1 dc in each dc to corner, 2 dc tog at corner, * miss 1 dc, [1 dc, 1 htr, 1 dc] in next dc, 1 ss in next dc, rep from * ending at top of band, 2 dc tog at corner, 1 dc in each dc, 1 ss in first st of shell on front edge. Fasten off.

Sew on buttons to match buttonholes.

Press as instructed on ball bands.

GILET WITH HOOD

QUICK TO MAKE IN DK YARN, WITH A COSY HOOD AND DRAWSTRING DETAILS.

SIZES

to fit chest	51	56	61 cm
	20	22	24 in
actual measurement	60	66	71 cm
	23½	26	28 in
length to shoulder	32	37	42 cm
	12½	14½	16½ in

MATERIALS

4 (5, 6) x 50 g balls of Sirdar Country Style DK in col.A (477 Russet Red)
1 (1, 1) x 50 g ball of Sirdar Country Style DK in col.B (411 Cream)
4.00 mm and 4.50 mm hooks
open-ended zip col. cream, length 25 (30, 35) cm (10 [12, 14] in)
narrow cord col. red, length 160 (170, 180) cm (63 [67, 71] in)
4 cord toggles or suitable beads

TENSION
7 patts and 12 rows to 10 cm (4 in) measured over Long and Short Stitch using size 4.50 mm hook.

BACK
Using size 4.50 mm hook and col.A make 44 (48, 52) ch.
foundation row (RS row): [1 tr, 1 htr] in 4th ch from hook, * miss 1 ch, [1 tr, 1 htr] in next ch, rep from * to end, turn. 21 (23, 25) patts.
Long and Short Stitch
row 1: 2 ch, * miss 1 patt, [1 tr, 1 htr] in sp before next patt, rep from * ending [1 tr, 1 htr] in 2 ch sp, turn.
Rep this row until Back measures 17.5 (20.5, 23.5) cm (7 [8, 9¼] in) ending with a WS row.

LONG AND SHORT STITCH

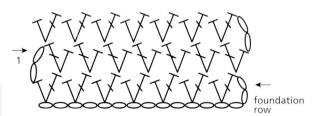

foundation row

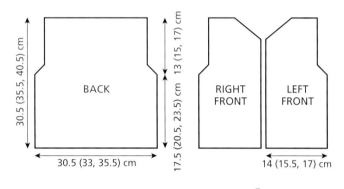

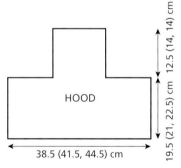

Shape Armholes
dec row 1: miss 1 htr, 1 ss in tr, 2 ch, patt as set to last patt, miss 1 htr, 1 htr in next tr, turn. 19 (21, 23) patts.
dec row 2: 2 ch, patt as set to last patt, miss 1 htr, 1 htr in next tr, turn. 18 (20, 22) patts.
Rep dec row 2, 5 more times. 13 (15, 17) patts.
Work in patt as set until Back measures 30.5 (35.5, 40.5) cm (12 [14, 16] in) in all. Fasten off.

LEFT FRONT
** Using size 4.50 mm hook and col.A make 22 (24, 26) ch.
Work foundation row and row 1 as for Back. 10(11, 12) patts.
Work in patt as set until Front measures 17.5 (20.5, 23.5) cm (7 [8, 9¼] in) ending with a WS row. **
Shape Armhole
dec row 1: miss 1 htr, 1 ss in tr, 2 ch, patt as set to end, turn. 9 (10, 11) patts.
dec row 2: 2 ch, patt as set to last patt, miss 1 htr, 1 htr in next tr, turn. 8 (9, 10) patts.
dec row 3: patt as set, turn.
Rep dec rows 2 and 3 twice more. 6 (7, 8) patts.

Work in patt as set until Front measures 25.5 (30.5, 35.5) cm (10 [12, 14] in) ending at front edge with a RS row.

Shape Neck

1st row: 2 ch, miss 1 patt, 1 htr in sp before next patt, patt as set to end, turn. 5 (6, 7) whole patts.

2nd row: 2 ch, patt as set to last complete patt, 1 htr in sp before patt, 1 htr in 2nd of 2 ch, turn. 4 (5, 6) patts.

Work 1st (1st and 2nd, 1st and 2nd) rows again. 3 (3, 4) patts.

Continue in patt as set until Front measures 30.5 (35.5, 40.5) cm (12 [14, 16] in) in all. Fasten off.

RIGHT FRONT

Work as given for Left Front from ** to **.

Shape Armhole

dec row 1: patt as set to last patt, miss 1 htr, 1 htr in next tr, turn. 9 (10, 11) patts.

dec row 2: 2 ch, patt as set to end, turn.

Rep these 2 rows 3 more times. 6 (7, 8) patts.

Work in patt as set until Front measures 25.5 (30.5, 35.5) cm (10 [12, 14] in) ending at armhole edge with a RS row.

Shape Neck

1st row: 2 ch, patt as set to last complete patt, 1 htr in sp before htr, 1 htr in 2nd of 2 ch, turn. 5 (6, 7) patts.

2nd row: 2 ch, miss 1 patt, 1 htr in sp before next patt, patt as set to end, turn. 4 (5, 6) patts.

Work 1st (1st and 2nd, 1st and 2nd) rows again. 3 (3, 4) patts. Continue in patt as set until Front measures 30.5 (35.5, 40.5) cm (12 [14, 16] in) in all. Fasten off.

HOOD

Join shoulder seams. With RS of work facing, using size 4.50 mm hook, join col.A at beg of neck shaping on Right Front.

row 1: 2 ch, [1 tr, 1htr] in same place 9 (9, 10) times up Right Front neck shaping rows to shoulder seam, 7 (9, 9) patts as set across Back neck edge, [1 tr, 1 htr] in same place 9 (9, 10) times down Left Front neck shaping rows working last patt under 2 ch at beg first neck shaping row, turn. 25 (27, 29) patts.

row 2: 2 ch, 8 (8, 9) patts as set, 2 patts in next sp, 7 (9, 9) patts as set, 2 patts in next sp, 8 (8, 9) patts as set to end. 27 (29, 31) patts.

Work in patt as set until Hood measures 19.5 (21, 22.5) cm (7¾ [8¼, 8¾] in) from neck edge. Fasten off.

next row: with same side of work facing, rejoin yarn to sp following 9th (10th, 10th) patt, 2 ch, 9 (9, 11) patts as set, turn,

leaving 9 (10, 10) patts unworked at end of row. Continue in patt for a further 12.5 (14, 14) cm (5 [5½, 5½] in). Fasten off.

Join seams at top of hood. Join underarm seams.

ARMHOLE BORDERS (make 2)

With RS of work facing, using size 4.00 mm hook, join col.B at top of underarm seam.

round 1: 1 ch, 3 dc in side edge of every 2 rows all round, ending 1 ss in first dc of round.

round 2: 1 ch, 1 dc in each dc ending 1 ss in first dc of round. Fasten off.

FRONT, NECK AND LOWER BORDER

Cut cord in half. Attach a toggle or bead to each cut end. With RS of work facing, using size 4.00 mm hook, join col.B at lower corner of Left Front.

round 1: 1 ch, 1 dc in base of each chain along lower edge to corner, 3 dc in same place at corner, 3 dc in side edge of every 2 rows up front edge, 1 dc in each st across top of Hood, 3 dc in side edge of every 2 rows ending 2 dc in same corner as first dc, 1 ss in first dc of round.

Do not work too tightly:

round 2: 1 ch, *1 dc over first cord and into next dc, rep from * ending in first dc of 3 at next corner, leave cord end at RS of work, 3 dc in next dc, 1 dc in each dc up Right Front edge to beg of neck shaping. Leaving second cord end at RS, work over second cord around edge of Hood to beg of neck shaping on Left Front, leave cord end at RS, 1 dc in each dc down Left Front edge ending 3 dc in last dc, 1 ss in first dc of round. Fasten off.

Pin and tack zip in place up Front edges, with last round of crochet just clear of the zip teeth. Use col.B or matching thread to backstitch each dc in place. At neck edge, fold ends of zip down underneath zip edging as neatly as possible.

Press as instructed on ball bands.

As an attractive variation, royal blue DK yarn (449) with matching blue cord for the drawstrings works well.

POLAR BEAR JACKET

A SIMPLE INTARSIA BEAR MOTIF AND ADD-ON
SNOWFLAKES DECORATE A SNUG JACKET TO KEEP OUT
WINTER CHILLS.

SIZES (see also page 58)

to fit chest	56	61	66 cm
	22	24	26 in
actual measurement	60	65	70 cm
	23¾	25½	27½ in
length to shoulder	34	39	44 cm
	13¼	15¼	17¼ in
sleeve seam with cuff	25	29	33 cm
folded back	9¾	11½	13 in

MATERIALS

4 (5, 6) x 50 g balls of Sirdar Country Style DK in col.A (429 Lupin)

1 (1, 1) x 50 g ball of Sirdar Country Style DK in col.B (412 White)

4.00 mm and 4.50 mm hooks

5 medium buttons

TENSION

16 sts and 12 rows to 10 cm (4 in) measured over rows of half trebles using size 4.50 mm hook.

Special Abbreviation: 1 rev dc: working from left to right (if you are right handed): insert hook into next dc to right with hook facing slightly downwards, catch yarn and pull through, turning hook back to normal position; yrh, pull through 2 lps on hook.

HALF TREBLE ROWS

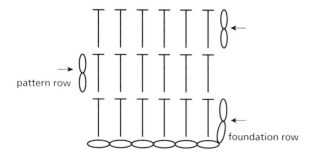

pattern row

foundation row

BACK

Using size 4.50 mm hook and col.A make 50 (54, 58) ch.
foundation row (RS row): 1 htr in 3rd ch from hook, 1 htr in each ch to end, turn. 48 (52, 56) htr.
patt row: 2 ch (do not count as a st), 1 htr in first htr, 1 htr in each htr to end, turn.
Rep patt row 6 (8, 12) more times. 8 (10, 14) rows in all.

Polar Bear Motif

Use Intarsia method (as page 13).

1st row: using col.A, 2 ch, 1 htr in first htr, 1 htr in each of next 6 (8, 10) htr, work 33 htr from row 1 of chart (reading right to left) in cols as shown, using col.A work 1 htr in each of 8 (10, 12) htr to end, turn.

2nd row: using col.A, 2 ch, 1 htr in first htr, 1 htr in each of next 7 (9, 11) htr, work 33 htr from row 2 of chart (reading left to right) in cols as shown, using col.A work 1 htr in each of last 7 (9, 11) htr, turn.

Continue in this way working successive chart rows until chart row 14 (16, 16) (WS row) is complete. Place a marker at each end of last row.

POLAR BEAR MOTIF

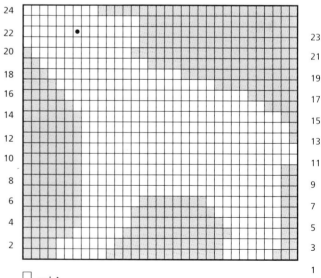

☐ col.A

▨ col.B

● french knot col.A

Shape Armholes

Continue reading from chart as set while shaping as follows:

dec row 1: 1 ch, miss first htr, 1 htr in each htr to last htr, miss last htr, turn.

Rep this row 3 more times ending chart row 18 (20, 20).

40 (44, 48) sts.

Work rem 6 (4, 4) chart rows in position as set.

Continue throughout in col.A. Rep patt row 6 (10, 12) times.

38 (44, 50) rows in all. Fasten off.

LEFT FRONT

** Using size 4.50 mm hook and col.A make 25 (27, 29) ch.

Work foundation row and patt row as for Back. 23 (25, 27) htr.

Rep patt row 20 (24, 28) more times. 22 (26, 30) rows in all. **

Place a marker at end of last row.

Shape Armhole

dec row 1: 1 ch, miss first htr, 1 htr in each htr to end, turn.

dec row 2: 2 ch, 1 htr in first htr, 1 htr in each htr to last htr, miss last htr, turn.

Rep these 2 rows once more.

19 (21, 23) htr.

Rep patt row 6 (8, 10) times.

32 (38, 44) rows in all.

Shape Front Neck

1st row: 2 ch, 1 htr in first htr, 1 htr in each of next 14 (15, 16) htr, turn.

2nd row: 1 ch, miss first htr, 1 htr in each htr to end, turn.

3rd row: 2 ch, 1 htr in first htr, 1 htr in each htr to last htr, miss last htr, turn.

4th row: as 2nd row. 12 (13, 14) htr.

Rep patt row twice. 38 (44, 50) rows in all. Fasten off.

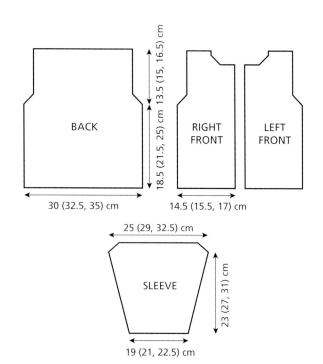

RIGHT FRONT

Work as given for Left Front from ** to **. Place a marker at beg of last row.

Shape Armhole

dec row 1: 2 ch, 1 htr in first htr, 1 htr in each htr to last htr, miss last htr, turn.

dec row 2: 1 ch, miss first htr, 1 htr in each htr to end, turn.

Rep these 2 rows once more. 19 (21, 23) htr.

Rep patt row 6 (8, 10) times. 32 (38, 44) rows. Fasten off.

Shape Neck

With RS of work facing, rejoin col.A to 4th (5th, 6th) htr.

1st row: 1 ch, 1 htr in next htr, 1 htr in each htr to end, turn.

2nd row: 2 ch, 1 htr in first htr, 1 htr in each htr to last htr, miss last htr, turn.

3rd row: 1 ch, miss first htr, 1 htr in each htr to end, turn.

4th row: as 2nd row. 12 (13, 14) htr.

Rep patt row twice. 38 (44, 50) rows in all. Fasten off.

SLEEVES (make 2)

Using size 4.00 mm hook and col.A make 32 (36, 38) ch.

Work foundation row and patt row as for Back. 30 (34, 36) htr.

2nd and 3rd Sizes Only

Rep patt row twice more.

All Sizes

2 (4, 4) rows.

Shape Sleeve

inc row 1: 2 ch, 1 htr in first htr, 1 htr in each htr to end, 1 htr in 2nd of 2 ch at beg of previous row, turn.

inc row 2: as inc row 1.

inc rows 3 and 4: as patt row. 32 (36, 38) htr. 6 (8, 8) rows.

Rep these 4 rows 4 (5, 7) more times. 40 (46, 52) htr.

22 (28, 36) rows.

Rep patt row until Sleeve measures 23 (27, 31) cm (9 [10½, 12¼] in) in all ending WS row. Place a marker at each end of last row.

Shape Top of Sleeve

dec row 1: 1 ch, miss first htr, 1 htr in each htr to last htr, miss last htr, turn.

Rep this row 3 more times. 32 (38, 44) htr. Fasten off.

TO FINISH

Join shoulder seams. Join top edges of Sleeves to armhole edges, matching markers and shaping rows. Join side and sleeve seams.

FRONT BANDS AND LOWER BORDER

With RS of work facing, using size 3.50 mm hook, join col.A at corner of Left Front neck shaping.

row 1: 1 ch, 3 dc in side edge of every 2 rows down front edge to

---

BACK — 18.5 (21.5, 25) cm / 13.5 (15, 16.5) cm — 30 (32.5, 35) cm

RIGHT FRONT — LEFT FRONT — 14.5 (15.5, 17) cm

SLEEVE — 25 (29, 32.5) cm / 23 (27, 31) cm / 19 (21, 22.5) cm

corner, 3 dc in same place at corner, 1 dc in base of each ch along lower edge to corner, 3 dc in same place at corner, 3 dc in side edge of every 2 rows up front edge ending at beg of neck shaping, turn.

row 2. 1 ch, 1 dc in first dc, 1 dc in each dc and 3 dc in 2nd of 3 dc at each corner, to end, turn.

to button left front over right: row 3: 1 ch, 1 dc in first dc, [2 ch, miss 2 dc, 1 dc in each of next 7 (8, 9) dc] 4 times, 2 ch, miss 2 dc, complete as row 2.

(to button right front over left: row 3: from top of Right Front count down 40 (44, 48) dc, place a marker on this st. Work as row 2 ending in marked st, [2 ch, miss 2 dc, 1 dc in each of next 7 (8, 9) dc] 4 times, 2 ch, miss 2 dc, 1 dc in last dc.)

both versions: row 4: as row 2, working 2 dc in each 2 ch sp. Fasten off.

Sew on buttons to match buttonholes.

COLLAR

With RS of work facing using size 4.00 mm hook join col.A to centre of top edge of Right Front Band.

1st row: 1 ch, 2 dc in top edge of band, 11 (13, 14) dc along front neck edge, 3 dc tog at back neck corner, 1 dc in each htr along back neck edge, 3 dc tog at corner, 11 (13, 14) dc along front neck edge and 2 dc along top edge of band to centre of band, turn.

2nd row: 1 ch, 1 dc in first dc, 1 dc in each dc to end, turn.

3rd row: 1 ch, 1 dc in first dc, * [2 dc in next dc, 1 dc in each of next 2 dc] 4 times, 2 dc in next dc *, 1 dc in each dc to last 14 dc, rep * to * once more, 1 dc in last dc, turn. 10 sts increased.

4th row: as 2nd row.

Rep this row 8 (10, 12) more times, without turning work on last row.

border row: 1 rev dc in each dc to end. Fasten off.

Left Side Collar Border

With RS of Collar facing, using size 3.50 mm hook join col.A at top corner of left front band: 1 ch, 1 dc in top edge of band, 3 dc tog at corner, 1 dc in side edge of each row of collar to corner. Fasten off.

Right Side Collar Border

Work as for Left Side Collar Border, beg at corner of collar and ending at corner of right front band.

CUFFS (make 2)

With RS of work facing, using size 3.50 mm hook join col.A at base of sleeve seam.

round 1: 1 ch, 1 dc in base of each ch ending 1 ss in first dc of round. 30 (34, 36) dc.

round 2: 1ch, 1 dc in first dc, 1 dc in each of next 4 (5, 6) dc, [2 dc tog over next 2 dc, 1 dc in each of next 4 (5, 5) dc] 3 times, 2 dc tog over next 2 dc, 1 dc in each dc to end of round.

round 3: 1 dc in each st of round.

Rep round 3, 6 more times ending 1 ss in 1 dc at underarm (level with sleeve seam).

border round: 1 rev dc in each dc, ending 1 ss in first rev dc of round. Fasten off.

SNOWFLAKE (make 14)

Using size 3.50 mm hook and col.B make 4 ch and join into a ring with 1 ss in first ch made.

round 1: (work over starting end of yarn) 2 ch, 1 tr into ring (first point made), * 2 ch, 1 ss through 2 front threads at top of point below, 2 ch, 2 tr tog into ring, rep from * 4 more times (6 points made), 2 ch, 1 ss through 2 front threads at top of point below, 2 ch, 1 ss in top of first point. Fasten off leaving a 25 cm (10 in) end.

Pull gently on starting end to tighten centre of snowflake. Secure and trim this end.

Arrange snowflakes on jacket following photograph as a guide: 3 on back, 5 on front and 3 on each sleeve. Use long end of yarn to stitch each snowflake in place.

Using col.A, work a french knot for polar bear's eye as shown on chart.

Optional: using col.B, work in chain stitch around outline of polar bear as shown in photograph.

Press as instructed on ball bands.

BIB PANTS

THE OPTIONAL TRACTOR MOTIF IS MADE SEPARATELY AND SEWN ON.

SIZES

to fit chest	51	56	61 cm
	20	22	24 in
to fit height	76–81	86–91	97–102 cm
	30–32	34–36	38–40 in
length to waist with cuff	40	45	50 cm
turned up	15¾	17¾	19½ in
inside leg	26	30	34 cm
	10¼	11¾	13¼ in

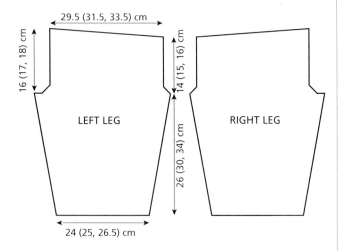

29.5 (31.5, 33.5) cm

16 (17, 18) cm

14 (15, 16) cm

LEFT LEG

RIGHT LEG

26 (30, 34) cm

24 (25, 26.5) cm

16 (18, 20) cm

17.5 (19.5, 21.5) cm

BIB

28.5 (30.5, 32.5) cm

MATERIALS

4 (5, 6) x 50 g balls of Sirdar Calypso 4-ply (4-ply cotton) in col.A (654 Classic Denim)
optional: oddments of DK cotton yarn: col.B (red) and col.C (black)
3.00 mm and 3.50 mm hooks
2 medium buttons
elastic 1 cm (½ in) wide, length to fit waist plus 2.5 cm (1 in)

TENSION

19 sts and 23 rows to 10 cm (4 in) measured over rows of double crochet using size 3.50 mm hook.

inc rows 3 and 4: as patt row. 48 (50, 52) dc. 8 (12, 14) rows.
Rep these 4 rows 10 (11, 12) more times. 68 (72, 76) dc.
48 (56, 62) rows.
Rep patt row until work measures 26 (30, 34) cm (10 [11¾, 13½] in) ending WS row. * Place a marker at end of last row.

Shape Crotch

1st row: 1 ch, 2 dc tog over first 2 dc, 1 dc in each dc to last 6 dc, 2 dc tog over next 2 dc, turn leaving last 4 dc unworked.

2nd row: 1 ch, 2 dc tog over 2 dc tog and first dc, 1 dc in each dc to last 2 sts, 2 dc tog over last dc and 2 dc tog, turn.
Rep 2nd row twice more. 56 (60, 64) sts.
Rep patt row until work measures 40 (45, 50) cm (15¾ [17¾, 19¾] in) in all ending RS row.

Shape Waist

waist row 1: 1 ch, 1 dc in first dc, 1 dc in each of next 36 (38, 40) dc, 1 ss in next dc, turn.

waist row 2: 1 dc in each dc to end, turn.

waist row 3: 1 ch, 1 dc in first dc, 1 dc in each of 17 (18, 19) dc, 1 ss in next dc, turn.

waist row 4: as waist row 2.

waist row 5: 1 ch, 1 dc in first dc, 1 dc in each dc and ss to end. Fasten off.

RIGHT LEG

Using size 3.50 mm hook and col.A make 47 (49, 51) ch.
foundation row (RS row): 1 dc in 2nd ch from hook, 1 dc in each ch to end, turn. 46 (48, 50) dc.
patt row: 1 ch, 1 dc in first dc, 1 dc in each dc to end, turn.
Rep patt row 2 (6, 8) more times. 4 (8, 10) rows in all.
Shape Leg
inc row 1: 1 ch, 2 dc in first dc, 1 dc in each dc to end, turn.
inc row 2: as inc row 1.

LEFT LEG

Work as Right Leg to *. Fasten off. Place a marker at beg of last row.
Shape Crotch
With RS of work facing, rejoin yarn to 4th dc of last row.
1st row: 1 ch, 2 dc tog over next 2 dc, 1 dc in each dc to last 2 dc, 2 dc tog over last 2 dc, turn.
2nd row: 1 ch, 2 dc tog over 2 dc tog and first dc, 1 dc in each dc to last 2 sts, 2 dc tog over last dc and 2 dc tog, turn.
Rep 2nd row twice more. 56 (60, 64) sts.

Rep patt row until length matches Right Leg at beg of waist shaping ending RS row.

Shape Waist

Work 1 WS row. Work waist rows 1–4 as for Right Leg. Fasten off.

WAISTBAND

Join centre front seam from waist edge down to markers. With RS of work facing, using size 3.50 mm hook, join yarn to first dc at waist edge.

row 1: 1 ch, 1 dc in first dc, 1 dc in each dc and ss to end, turn. 112 (120, 128) dc.

row 2: 1 ch, 1 dc in back lp only (as work faces you) of each dc to end, turn.

rows 3–6: as patt row. Fasten off.

With WS of work facing, rejoin yarn to empty front lp of first dc of row 2, 2 ch, *1 tr in next front lp, 1 ch, miss 1 front loop, rep from * to end, turn.

next row: work through both thicknesses to form casing for elastic: 1 ch, 1 dc in back lp of first dc of row 6 together with front lp of first tr behind, * 1 dc in back lp of next dc together with front lp of ch behind, 1 dc in back lp of next dc together with front lp of tr behind, rep from * working last dc together with 2nd of 2 ch behind. Fasten off.

BIB

With RS of work facing using size 3.50 mm hook rejoin col.A to 29th (31st, 33rd) dc of last row of Waistband.

row 1: 1 ch, 1 dc in next dc, 1 dc in each of next 52 (56, 60) dc, 2 dc tog over next 2 dc, turn. 54 (58, 62) sts.

row 2: 1 ch, 2 dc tog over 2 dc tog and next dc, 1 dc in each dc to last 2 sts, 2 dc tog over last dc and 2 dc tog, turn. 52 (56, 60) sts. Rep row 2, 8 more times. 36 (40, 44) sts.

next row: 1 ch, 1 dc in 2 dc tog, 1 dc in each dc ending 1 dc in 2 dc tog, turn.

foll row: 1 ch, 2 dc tog over first 2 dc, 1 dc in each dc to last 2 dc, 2 dc tog over last 2 dc, turn. 34 (38, 42) sts. Rep these 2 rows twice more. 30 (34, 38) sts. Rep patt row until Bib measures 10 (12, 13.5) cm (4 [4¾, 5¼] in) from top of Waistband, ending WS row.

Shape Neck: First Side

1st row: 1 ch, 1 dc in first dc, 1 dc in each of next 9 dc, 2 dc tog over next 2 dc, turn.

2nd row: 1 ch, 2 dc tog over 2 dc tog and next dc, 1 dc in each dc to end, turn.

3rd row: 1 ch, 1 dc in first dc, 1 dc in each dc to last dc and 2 dc tog, 2 dc tog over last 2 sts, turn.

4th row: as 2nd row. 8 sts.

** Rep patt row until Bib measures 17 (19, 21) cm (6½ [7½, 8¼] in) from top of Waistband ending WS row.

next row: 1 ch, 2 dc tog over first 2 dc, 1 dc in each of 4 dc, 2 dc tog over last 2 dc. Fasten off.

Second Side

With RS of Bib facing, leave 5 (9, 13) dc at centre front, using size 3.50 mm hook rejoin col.A to next dc.

1st row: 1 ch, 2 dc tog over next 2 dc, 1 dc in each of 10 dc to end, turn.

2nd row: 1 ch, 1 dc in first dc, 1 dc in each dc to last dc and 2 dc tog, 2 dc tog over last 2 sts, turn.

3rd row: 1 ch, 2 dc tog over 2 dc tog and next dc, 1 dc in each dc to end, turn.

4th row: as 2nd row. Complete as First Side from ** to end.

FIRST STRAP

With RS of work facing, using size 3.50 mm hook rejoin col.A to 10th (11th, 12th) dc of last row of Waistband.

*** row 1: 1 ch, 1 dc in each of next 8 dc, turn.
Rep patt row until Strap measures 20 (22, 24) cm (7¾ [8½, 9½] in), or length required. (Note: straps are worn crossed at centre back.)
buttonhole row: 1 ch, 1 dc in each of first 3 dc, 2 ch, miss 2 dc, 1 dc in each of 3 dc to end, turn.
foll row: as patt row working 2 dc in 2 ch sp.
Rep patt row once more.
next row: 1 ch, 2 dc tog over first 2 dc, 1 dc in each of 4 dc, 2 dc tog over last 2 dc. Fasten off.

SECOND STRAP

With RS of work facing, using size 3.50 mm hook rejoin col.A to 10th (11th, 12th) dc after Bib along last row of Waistband. Complete as First Strap from *** to end.

TO FINISH

Join centre back seam and inside leg seams.

BIB AND STRAP BORDER

With RS of work facing, using size 3.00 mm hook, join col.A at top of centre back seam.
round 1: 1 ch, 1 dc in each dc along Waistband to corner of Strap, 3 dc tog at corner, 1 dc in side edge of each row to end of strap, [2 dc in 2 dc tog, 1 dc in each dc, 2 dc in 2 dc tog] across end of Strap, 1 dc in side edge of each row to corner, 3 dc tog at corner, 1 dc in each dc to base of Bib, 1 dc in side edge of each row to top of shoulder, work across top of shoulder in same way as top of Strap, 1 dc in side edge of each row down neck shaping, 2 dc tog at corner, 1 dc in each dc across centre front, 2 dc tog at corner, then complete the second half of edging in same way as first half, ending 1 ss in first dc of round at centre back. Fasten off.

ANKLE CUFFS (make 2)

With RS of work facing, using size 3.00 mm hook join col.A at base of inside leg seam.
round 1: 1 ch, 1 dc in base of each ch, ending 1 dc in first dc of round.
round 2: 1 dc in each dc all round.
Rep round 2, 4 more times ending 1 ss in 1 dc at inside leg. Fasten off.

TRACTOR MOTIF

Special Abbreviation: 1 ddtr: 1 double double treble worked as follows: yrh 3 times, insert hook as directed, yrh, pull through work only, [yrh, pull through 2 lps] 4 times.
Body (follow chart above)
Using size 3.50 mm hook and col.B make 9 ch.
row 1: 1 dc in 2nd ch from hook, 1 dc in each ch to end, turn. 8 dc.
row 2: 2 ch, 1 dc in each dc to end, turn.
row 3: 2 ch, 1 dc in each dc , ending 2 dc under 2 ch, turn. 10 dc.
row 4: 3 ch, 1 dc in 2nd ch from hook, 1 dc in next ch, 1 dc in each dc ending 2 dc under 2 ch, turn.14 dc.
row 5: 4 ch, 1 dc in 3rd ch from hook, 1 dc in next ch, 1 dc in each dc to end, turn. 16 dc.
row 6: 1 ch, 1 dc in each dc ending 1 dc under 2 ch, turn. 17 dc.
row 7: 6 ch, miss first 3 dc, 1 ddtr in next dc, 3 ch, miss 4 dc, 1 ddtr in next dc, turn.
row 8: 2 ch, 1 dc in ddtr, 1 dc in each of 3 ch, 1 dc in ddtr, 1 dc in each of next 2 ch, 2 dc in next ch. Fasten off leaving a long end.

TRACTOR BODY

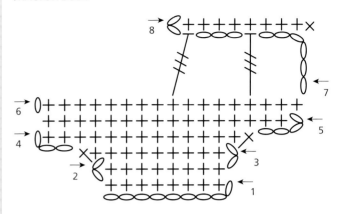

SMALL WHEEL

LARGE WHEEL

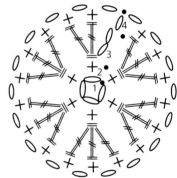

 = 3 trebles in back loop

Large Wheel (follow chart above)
Using size 3.50 mm hook and col.B make 4 ch and join into a ring with 1 ss in first ch made.
round 1: (work over starting end) 6 dc into ring, 1 ss in first dc of round. Fasten off.
Join col.C to back lp only of first dc.
round 2: (work over both yarn ends) 2 ch, 2 tr in back lp of same dc, 3 tr in back lp of each of next 5 dc, 1 ss in 2nd of 2 ch at beg of round.
round 3: 2 ch, *1 dc in next tr, 1 ch, rep from * ending 1 ss in first of 2 ch. Fasten off leaving a long end.
Small Wheel (follow chart above)
Work as Large Wheel to end of round 2. Fasten off leaving a long end.
Use the long ends to sew Body and Wheels to Bib following the photograph as a guide, backstitching around the edge of each piece.
Sew buttons to front shoulders, to match buttonholes on Straps. With straps crossed at centre back and buttoned to front, backstitch around the crossover in a diamond shape. Thread elastic through casing at waist, overlap the ends by 2.5 cm (1 in) and oversew securely.
Ankle Cuffs may be worn folded up or down.
Press as instructed on ball bands.

FLOWER MOTIF TOP AND BAG

COOL AND PRETTY, WITH A MATCHING BAG.

SIZES

TOP

to fit chest	51	56	61 cm
	20	22	24 in
actual measurement	57	63	69 cm
	22½	24¾	27 in
length to shoulder	31.5	37.5	41.5 cm
	12½	14¾	16¼ in
sleeve seam	4.5	5.5	6.5 cm
	1¾	2¼	2½ in

BAG

12.5 cm (5 in) square

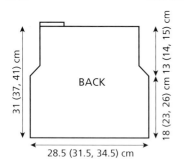

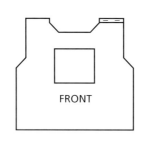

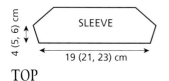

TOP

BACK
Using size 3.50 mm hook and col.A make 59 (65, 71) ch.

foundation row (RS row): 1 tr in 4th ch from hook, 1 tr in each ch to end, turn. 57 (63, 69) sts. (First 3 ch counts as first st.)

treble row: 3 ch, miss first tr, 1 tr in each tr, ending 1 tr in 3rd of 3 ch, turn. *

Rep this row 16 (21, 24) more times. 18 (23, 26) rows in all. Place a marker at each end of last row.

Shape Armholes
dec row 1: 2 ch, miss first tr, 2 tr tog over next 2 trs, 1 tr in each tr to last tr and 3 ch, 2 tr tog over last 2 sts, turn. 55 (61, 67) sts.

dec row 2: 2 ch, miss 2 tr tog, 2 tr tog over next 2 sts, 1 tr in each tr to last 2 tr tog and 2 ch, 2 tr tog over last 2 sts, turn. 53 (59, 65) sts.

Rep dec row 2, twice more. 49 (55, 61) sts.

Work 9 (10, 11) more treble rows, without shaping. 31 (37, 41) rows in all, ending RS row.

MATERIALS

FOR THE SET
4 (4, 5) x 50 g balls of Patons Crystal (DK acrylic microfibre) in col.A (02673 Blossom)
1 (1, 1) x 50 g ball of Patons Crystal (DK acrylic microfibre) in col.B (02671 Cream)
3.00 mm and 3.50 mm hooks
2 buttons for Top, 1 button for Bag

TENSION
20 sts and 10 rows to 10 cm (4 in) measured over rows of trebles using size 3.50 mm hook.

MOTIF

↗ 1 ss into edge of opening

Change to size 3.00 mm hook.

Button Border
next row: 1 ch, 1 dc in first tr, 1 dc in each of next 14 (16, 18) tr, turn.

foll row: 1 ch, 1 dc in each dc to end, turn. Rep this row twice more. Fasten off.

FRONT

Work as given for Back to *.

Rep treble row 11 (16, 19) more times. 13 (18, 21) rows in all, ending RS (WS, RS) row.

Opening for Motif: First Side

next row: 3 ch, miss first tr, 1 tr in each of next 17 (20, 23) trs, turn. 18 (21, 24) sts.

Work 4 more rows on these sts only ending at edge of opening. 18 (23, 26) rows in all. Place a marker at side edge of last row.

Shape Armhole

dec row 1: 3 ch, miss first tr, 1 tr in each tr to last tr and 3 ch, 2 tr tog over last 2 sts, turn. 17 (20, 23) sts.

dec row 2: 2 ch, miss 2 tr tog, 2 tr tog over next 2 sts, 1 tr in each tr ending 1 tr in 3rd of 3 ch, turn. 16 (19, 22) sts.

dec row 3: 3 ch, miss first tr, 1 tr in each tr to last 2 tr tog and 2 ch, 2 tr tog over last 2 sts, turn. 15 (18, 21) sts.

dec row 4: as dec row 2. 14 (17, 20) sts.

Work 1 more treble row. 23 (28, 31) rows in all, ending RS (WS, RS) row. Fasten off.

Second Side

Leave 21 tr at centre front and rejoin col.A to next tr.

next row: 3 ch, 1 tr in each tr ending 1 tr in 3rd of 3 ch, turn. 18 (21, 24) sts.

Work 4 more rows on these sts. 18(23, 26) rows in all. Place a marker at side edge of last row.

Shape Armhole

dec row 1: 2 ch, miss first tr, 2 tr tog over next 2 trs, 1 tr in each tr ending 1 tr in 3rd of 3 ch, turn. 17 (20, 23) sts.

dec row 2: 3 ch, miss first tr, 1 tr in each tr to last 2 tr tog and 2 ch, 2 tr tog over last 2 sts, turn. 16 (19, 22) sts.

dec row 3: 2 ch, miss 2 tr tog, 2 tr tog over next 2 sts, 1 tr in each tr ending 1 tr in 3rd of 3 ch, turn. 15 (18, 21) sts.

dec row 4: as dec row 2. 14 (17, 20) sts.

Work 1 more treble row. 23 (28, 31) rows in all, ending RS (WS, RS) row.

Work 21 ch. Fasten off with 1 ss in top corner at opposite side of opening.

Complete Square Opening

With WS (RS, WS) of work facing, rejoin col.A to last tr of last row of First Side.

next row: 3 ch, miss first tr, 1 tr in each of 13 (16, 19) trs, 1 tr in each of 21 ch, 1 tr in each of 13 (16, 19) trs, 1 tr in 3rd of 3 ch, turn. 49 (55, 61) sts.

Work 2 (3, 4) more Treble rows. 26 (32, 36) rows in all ending WS row.

Shape Neck: First Side

1st row: 3 ch, miss first tr, 1 tr in each of next 16 (18, 20) trs, 2 tr tog over next 2 trs, turn. 18 (20, 22) sts.

2nd row: 2 ch, miss 2 tr tog, 2 tr tog over next 2 trs, 1 tr in each tr ending 1 tr in 3rd of 3 ch, turn. 17 (19, 21) sts.

3rd row: 3 ch, miss first tr, 1 tr in each tr to last 2 tr tog and 2 ch, 2 tr tog over last 2 sts, turn. 16 (18, 20) sts.

4th row: as 2nd row. 15 (17, 19) sts. 30 (36, 40) rows in all ending WS row.

Buttonhole Border

Change to size 3.00 mm hook.

1st row: 1 ch, 1 dc in first tr, 1 dc in each of next 14 (16, 18) sts, turn.

2nd row: 1 ch, 1 dc in first dc, 1 dc in each dc to end, turn.

3rd row: 1 ch, 1 dc in first dc, 1 dc in each of next 4 (5, 6) dc, 2 ch, miss 2 dc, 1 dc in each of next 5 (6, 7) dc, 2 ch, miss 2 dc, 1 dc in last dc, turn.

4th row: 1 ch, 1 dc in first dc, 2 dc in each 2 ch sp and 1 dc in each dc to end. Fasten off.

Second Side

With RS of Front facing, leave 11 (13, 15) trs at centre front. Using size 3.50 mm hook rejoin col.A to next tr.

1st row: 2 ch, 2 tr tog over next 2 trs, 1 tr in each tr ending 1 tr in 3rd of 3 ch, turn. 18 (20, 22) sts.

2nd row: 3 ch, miss first tr, 1 tr in each tr to last 2 tr tog and 2 ch, 2 tr tog over last 2 sts, turn. 17 (19, 21) sts.

3rd row: 2 ch, miss 2 tr tog, 2 tr tog over next 2 trs, 1 tr in each tr ending 1 tr in 3rd of 3 ch, turn. 16 (18, 20) sts.

4th row: as 2nd row.

Work 1 treble row on these sts. 31 (37, 41) rows in all ending RS row. Fasten off.

Border of Square Opening

With RS of Front facing,

using size 3.00 mm hook, join col.A to first tr at lower right corner of opening.

edging round: 1 ch, 1 dc in each of next 19 trs, 2 dc tog at corner, 19 dc evenly spaced up side edge ending 2 dc tog at next corner, 1 dc in base of each of next 19 ch, 2 dc tog at next corner, 19 dc evenly spaced down side edge ending 1 ss under 1 ch at beg of round. Fasten off.

Motif

Worked in rounds:

Using size 3.50 mm hook and col.B, make 4 ch and join into a ring with 1 ss in first ch made.

round 1: (work over starting end of yarn) 1 ch, 8 dc into ring, 1 ss into first dc of round. Fasten off. Join col.A to next dc.

round 2: 4 ch, 2 dtr tog into dc at base of these 4 ch, * 4 ch, 3 dtr tog in next dc, rep from * ending 4 ch, 1 ss in top of 2 dtr tog. Fasten off. Rejoin col.A to same place.

round 3: 4 ch, 1 dc in st at base of these 4 ch, * [4 dc in next 4 ch sp, 1 dc in top of next group] twice, 3 ch, 1 dc in st at base of these 3 ch, rep from * twice more, 4 dc in next 4 ch sp, 1 dc in top of next group, 4 dc in next 4 ch sp, 1 ss in first of 4 ch at beg of round.

round 4: * [1 dc, 3 ch, 1 dc] in corner lp, 5 ch, miss 5 dc, 1 dc in next dc, 5 ch, miss 5 dc, rep from * ending 1 ss in first dc of round.

round 5: * [1 dc, 5 ch, 1 dc] in corner lp, 5 ch, miss 1 dc and 2 ch, 1 dc in next ch, 5 ch, miss [2 ch, 1 dc, 2 ch], 1 dc in next ch, 5 ch, miss 2 ch and 1 dc, rep from * ending 1 ss in first dc of round. Change to size 3.00 mm hook. Join motif into opening with right sides of Front and Motif facing you:

round 6: * 3 dc in corner lp, 1 ss in 2 dc tog at one corner of opening (inserting hook from back through to front), 3 dc in same corner lp, [3 dc in next 5 ch sp, miss 4 dc along edge of opening, 1 ss through next dc, 3 dc in same 5 ch sp] 3 times, rep from * ending 1 ss in first dc of round. Fasten off.

Pull gently on starting end of yarn to tighten centre of Motif.

SLEEVES (make 2)

Using size 3.50 mm hook and col.A make 40 (44, 48) ch. Work foundation row and treble row as for Back. 38 (42, 46) sts. Rep treble row 1 (2, 3) more times. 3 (4, 5) rows.

inc row: 3 ch, 1 tr in first tr, 1 tr in each tr ending 2 tr in 3rd of 3 ch, turn. 40 (44, 48) tr. Place a marker at each end of last row.

Shape Top of Sleeve

dec row 1: 2 ch, miss first tr, 2 tr tog over next 2 tr, 1 tr in each tr to last 2 tr and 3 ch, 2 tr tog over last 2 tr, miss top of 3 ch, turn. 36 (40, 44) sts.

dec row 2: 2 ch, miss 2 tr tog, 2 tr tog over next 2 tr, 1 tr in each tr to last 2 tr, 2 tr tog over last 2 tr, miss 2 tr tog and top of 2 ch, turn. 32 (36, 40) sts.

Rep dec row 2 twice more. 24 (28, 32) sts. Fasten off.

TO FINISH

Join right shoulder seam.

Neck Border

With right side of work facing, using size 3.00 mm hook, join col.A to neck edge at corner of Buttonhole Border.

row 1: work in dc all round neck edge, working 1 dc in side edge of each row of border, 2 dc in side edge of each row of trebles, 1 dc in each tr and 2 dc tog at each inside corner, up to corner of Button Border, turn.

row 2: 1 ch, 1 dc in first dc, 1 dc in each dc to end, working 2 dc tog at each inside corner. Fasten off.

Lap Buttonhole Border over Button Border and sew down at armhole edge.

Sew top edges of sleeves to armhole edges, stretching slightly to fit between markers.

Join sleeve seams. Join side seams, leaving lowest 5 rows unstitched at each side.

Sleeve Border (make 2)

With RS of work facing, using size 3.00 mm hook and col.A, join yarn to base of sleeve seam.

round 1: 1 ch, 1 dc in base of each ch all round, ending 1 ss in first dc of round. Fasten off.

Lower Border

With RS of work facing, using size 3.00 mm hook, join col.A to one corner of lower edge.

round 1: 1 ch, work all round in dc: 1 dc in base of each ch along lower edges, 3 dc in same place at each outer corner, 2 dc in side edge of each row of side splits, 3 dc tog at top of each side split, ending at first corner with 2 dc in same place as first st, 1 ss in first dc of round. Fasten off.

Sew on buttons to match buttonholes.

Press as instructed on ball bands.

BAG

FRONT AND BACK (make 2)

Using size 3.50 mm hook work rounds 1–3 of Motif as for Front of Top.

round 4: 1 ss in 3 ch sp, 5 ch, 1 tr in same 3 ch sp, * 1 tr in each of 11 dc, [1 tr, 3 ch, 1 tr] in 3 ch sp, rep from * twice more, 1 tr in each of 11 dc, 1 ss in 2nd of 5 ch at beg of round.

round 5: 1 ss in 3 ch sp, 5 ch, 1 tr in same 3 ch sp, * 1 tr in each of 13 tr, [1 tr, 3 ch, 1 tr] in 3 ch sp, rep from * twice more, 1 tr in each of 13 tr, 1 ss in 2nd of 5 ch at beg of round.

round 6: 1 ss in 3 ch sp, 5 ch, 1 tr in same 3 ch sp, * 1 tr in each of 15 tr, [1 tr, 3 ch, 1 tr] in 3 ch sp, rep from * twice more, 1 tr in each of 15 tr, 1 ss in 2nd of 5 ch at beg of round. Fasten off.

TO FINISH

Place Front and Back with WS together. Using size 3.00 mm hook join col.A to both 3 ch sps at one corner.

edging round: make 110 ch for Strap (or length required), 2 dc in both 3 ch sps at next corner, work through both thicknesses: * 1 dc in each of next 17 tr, [2 dc, 2 ch, 2 dc] in 3 ch sp at next corner, rep from * once more, 1 dc in each of next 17 tr, 2 dc in 3 ch sp at base of strap, 1 dc in each of 110 ch, 1 ss in first dc at next corner. Fasten off.

Edge of Opening

With RS of Back facing using size 3.00 mm hook join col.A to 9th of 17 tr along open edge, 7 ch, 1 ss in tr at base of these 7 ch, 1 dc in each of next 8 tr, 1 dc in 3 ch sp, 1 ss in base of Strap, turn and work along other edge of opening: 1 dc in 3 ch sp, 1 dc in each of 17 tr, 1 dc in 3 ch sp, 1 ss in base of Strap, turn and complete first edge: 1 dc in 3 ch sp, 1 dc in each of 8 tr, 1 dc in tr at base of ch lp, 10 dc into lp, 1 ss in next dc. Fasten off.

Sew on button to match loop. Press as instructed on ball bands.

PINAFORE

FRESH AND PRETTY IN COOL COTTON, TO WEAR BY ITSELF OR OVER A T-SHIRT.

SIZES

to fit chest	51	56	61 cm
	20	22	24 in
actual measurement	51	57	63 cm
at underarm	20	22½	24¾ in
length to shoulder	43	48	53 cm
	17	19	21 in

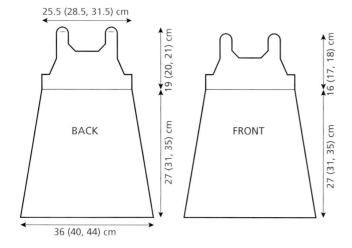

MATERIALS

9 (10, 11) x 25 g balls of Twilleys Lyscordet (4 ply cotton) in col.A (78 White)
1 (1, 1) x 25 g ball of Twilleys Lyscordet (4 ply cotton) in col.B (87 Pale Pink)
2.50 mm and 3.00 mm hooks
2 buttons

TENSION
Using size 3.00 mm hook: 26 sts and 26 rows to 10 cm (4 in) measured over Bushy Stitch as for Bodice; 7½ patts and 16 rows to 10 cm (4 in) measured over Star Pattern as for Skirt.

BACK
Bodice
Using size 3.00 mm hook and col.A make 68 (76, 84) ch.
foundation row: miss 3 ch, * 2 dc in next ch, miss 1 ch, rep from * ending 2 dc in last ch, turn.
Bushy Stitch
pattern row: 2 ch, * miss 1 dc, 2 dc in next dc, rep from * to end, turn. 33 (37, 41) patts.
Rep this row 4 (6, 8) more times. 6 (8, 10) rows in all.

BUSHY STITCH

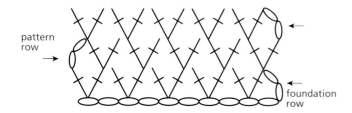

pattern row →

→ foundation row

Shape Armholes
1st dec row: ss across first 4 dc, 1 ch, [miss 1 dc, 2 dc in next dc] 28 (32, 36) times, miss 1 dc, 1 dc in next dc, turn, leaving last 4 dc unworked.
2nd dec row: 1 ch, miss 2 dc, * 2 dc in next dc, miss 1 dc, rep from * ending miss last dc, 1 dc in 1 ch, turn.
3rd dec row: 1 ch, miss 2 dc, * 2 dc in next dc, miss 1 dc, rep from * ending 1 dc in last dc, turn.
Rep 3rd dec row, 7 (9, 11) more times. 19 (21, 23) patts.
next row: 2 ch, miss 2 dc, * 2 dc in next dc, miss 1 dc, rep from * ending 2 dc in last dc, turn. **
Rep Bushy Stitch patt row until work measures 5 cm (2 in) from last shaping row, ending WS row.
Shape Back Neck: First Side
1st row: 2 ch, [miss 1 dc, 2 dc in next dc] 6 times, miss 1 dc, 1 dc in next dc, turn.
2nd row: 1 ch, miss 2 dc, patt as set to end, turn.
3rd row: 2 ch, * miss 1 dc, 2 dc in next dc, rep from * to last 2 dc, miss 1 dc, 1 dc in last dc, turn.
4th row: as 2nd row.
5th and 6th rows: as 3rd and 2nd. 4 patts.
*** Work in patt until Bodice measures 17 (18, 19) cm (6¾ [7, 7½] in) in all ending WS row.
buttonhole row: 2 ch, miss 1 dc, 3 dc in next dc, 2 ch, miss 5 dc, 3 dc in last dc, turn.
foll row: 2 ch, * miss 1 st, 2 dc in next st, rep from * to end, turn.
last row: 1 ch, miss 1 dc, 1 dc in next dc, [miss 1 dc, 2 dc in next dc] twice, miss 1 dc, 1 ss in next dc. Fasten off.
Second Side
With right side of work facing, leave 11 (13, 15) dc at centre front and rejoin col.A to next dc.
1st row: 1 ch, miss 1 dc, [2 dc in next dc, miss 1 dc] 5 times, 2 dc in

last dc, turn.

2nd row: 2 ch, [miss 1 dc, 2 dc in next dc] 5 times, miss 1 dc, 1 dc in next dc, turn.

3rd row: 1 ch, miss 2 dc, 2 dc in next dc, patt as set to end, turn.

4th row: 2 ch, [miss 1 dc, 2 dc in next dc] 4 times, miss 1 dc, 1 dc in next dc, turn.

5th row: as 3rd row.

6th row: 2 ch, [miss 1 dc, 2 dc in next dc] 4 times, turn.
Work as first side from *** to end.

Skirt

With right side of work facing, using size 3.00 mm hook, join col.A to base loop of first ch made.

preparation row: Work in base loops of foundation chain: 2 ch, 2 tr in lp at base of these 2 ch, * miss 1 ch, [1 dc, 2 tr] in next ch, miss 2 ch, [1 dc, 2 tr] in next ch, rep from * to last 4 (2, -) sts, then:

1st size only: * miss 1 ch, [1 dc, 2 tr] in next ch, rep from * once, 1 dc in base of 3 ch at beg row 1 of bodice, turn.

2nd size only: miss 1 ch, [1 dc, 2 tr] in next ch, 1 dc in base of 3 ch at beg row 1 of bodice, turn.

3rd size only: 1 dc in base of 3 ch at beg row 1 of bodice, turn.

All Sizes

27 (30, 33) patts.

Star Pattern

row 1: 2 ch, 2 tr in dc at base of these 2 ch, * miss 2 tr, [1 dc, 2 tr] in next dc, rep from * ending miss 2 tr, 1 dc in 2nd of 2 ch at beg previous row, turn.

Rep this row until Skirt measures 29 (33, 37) cm (11½ [13, 14½] in), or length required, ending WS row. Fasten off.

STAR PATTERN

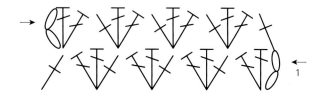

FRONT

Bodice

Work as given for Back to **.
Work 1 patt row, thus ending WS row.

Shape Front Neck: First Side

Work 1st–6th rows as given for first side of back neck shaping.
**** Work in patt until bodice measures 16 (17, 18) cm (6¼ [6¾, 7] in) in all.

last row: 1 ch, miss 1 dc, 1 dc in next dc, [miss 1 dc, 2 dc in next dc] twice, miss 1 dc, 1 ss in next dc. Fasten off.

Second Side

With right side of work facing, leave 11 (13, 15) dc at centre front and rejoin col.A to next dc.
Work 1st–6th rows as given for second side of back neck shaping.
Work as first side from **** to end.

Skirt

Work as given for Back.

TO FINISH

Join side seams by slip stitching on wrong side, matching row ends.

Neck and Armhole Border

With right side of work facing, using size 2.50 mm hook, join col.A at left underarm seam, 1 ch, then work all round top edge in dc, working 1 dc in each st and 1 dc in side edge of each row, with 3 dc in same place at top corners of each strap, ending 1 ss under 1 ch at beg of round.

edging round: * [1 ss, 1 ch, 1 dc] in next dc, miss 1 dc, rep from * ending 1 ss under first ch of round. (If necessary, end 1 ss, 1 ch, 2 dc tog over last 2 dc, 1 ss under first ch of round.) Fasten off.
Sew a button to the front of each shoulder to correspond with the buttonholes.

Lower Border

With right side of work facing, using size 2.50 mm hook and col.A, join yarn to base of one side seam, 1 ch, then work 1 dc in each tr and 1 ss in each dc, all round lower edge, ending 1 ss under 1 ch at beg of round. Fasten off.

Flower (make about 20)

Using size 2.50 mm hook and col.B, make 5 ch and join into a ring with 1 ss in first ch made.

round 1: (work over starting end of yarn) 1 ch, 10 dc into ring, 1 ss under 1 ch at beg of round.

round 2: * 2 ch, 3 tr in next dc, 2 ch, 1 ss in next dc, rep from * 4 more times ending with last ss in dc at base of 2 ch. Fasten off leaving about 25 cm (10 in) end.

Pull gently on starting end of yarn to tighten centre of flower. Run in this end.

Arrange half the flowers on the front of the pinafore and half on the back, following the photograph as a guide. Use the long end of yarn to stitch down each flower with tiny backstitches around the centre circle.

Press as instructed on ball bands.

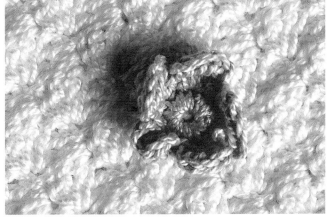

71

TARTAN CROPPED JACKET AND BERET

TRY THE TECHNIQUE OF WOVEN CROCHET: THE GARMENT PIECES
ARE WORKED WITH A PATTERN GRID OF MESH HOLES, THEN THE
CONTRASTING COLOURS ARE WOVEN THROUGH THE MESH.

SIZES

JACKET

to fit chest	51	56	61 cm
	20	22	24 in
actual measurement	58	64	71 cm
	23	25	28 in
length to shoulder	26	29	34 cm
	10¼	11½	13¼ in
sleeve seam with	20	25	28.5 cm
cuff folded back	8	9¾	11¼ in

BERET

to fit head	45.5	48	50.5 cm
	18	19	20 in

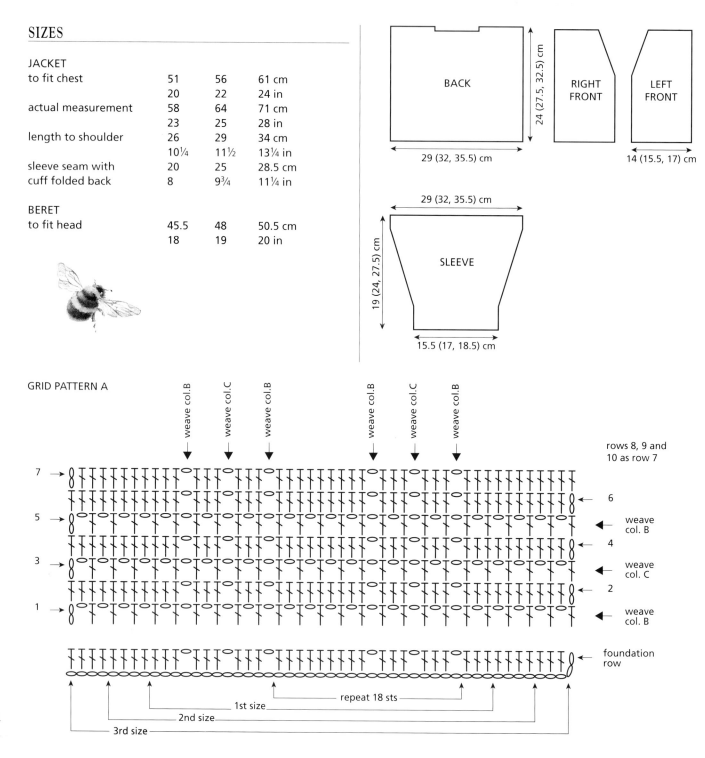

GRID PATTERN A

72

MATERIALS

FOR THE SET:
3 (4, 4) x 50 g balls of Jaeger Matchmaker Merino 4-ply in col.A (697 Peony)
1 (1, 1) x 50 g ball of Jaeger Matchmaker Merino 4-ply in col.B (713 Meadow)
1 (1, 1) x 50 g ball of Jaeger Matchmaker Merino 4-ply in col.C (740 Baltic Blue)
2.50 mm and 3.00 mm hooks
blunt-ended tapestry needle for weaving
4 buttons for jacket

TENSION
JACKET: 24 sts and 12 rows to 10 cm (4 in) measured over Grid Pattern using size 3.00 mm hook.
BERET: First 8 rounds should measure 10 cm (4 in) in diameter.

Special Abbreviation: 1 rev dc: working from left to right (if you are right-handed): insert hook into next dc to right with hook facing slightly downwards, catch yarn and pull through, turning hook back to normal position; yrh, pull through 2 lps on hook.

JACKET

Grid Pattern A
row 1: 3 ch, miss first 2 tr, * 1 tr in next tr, 1 ch, miss 1 st (which may be 1 tr or 1 ch), rep from * ending 1 tr in 2nd of 2 ch at beg previous row, turn.
row 2: 2 ch, miss first tr, [1 tr in 1 ch sp, 1 tr in next tr] 1 (3, 5) times, * [1 ch, miss 1 ch, 1 tr in next tr, 1 tr in 1 ch sp, 1 tr in next tr] twice, 1 ch, miss 1 ch, [1 tr in next tr, 1 tr in 1 ch sp] 4 times, 1 tr in next tr, rep from * ending [1 tr in next tr, 1 tr in 1 ch sp] 1 (3, 5) times, 1 tr in 2nd of 3 ch, turn.
rows 3–6: as rows 1 and 2, twice.
row 7: 2 ch, miss first tr, 1 tr in each of next 2 (6, 10) tr, * [1 ch, miss 1 ch, 1 tr in each of next 3 tr] twice, 1 ch, miss 1 ch, 1 tr in each of next 9 tr, rep from * ending 1 tr in each of 2 (6, 10) tr, 1 tr in 2nd of 2 ch, turn.
rows 8, 9 and 10: as row 7.
These 10 rows form Grid Pattern A. Repeat them as given below.

BACK
Using size 3.00 mm hook and col.A make 70 (78, 86) ch.
foundation row (RS row): 1 tr in 3rd ch from hook, 1 tr in each of next 1 (5, 9) ch, * [1 ch, miss 1 ch, 1 tr in each of next 3 ch] twice, 1 ch, miss 1 ch, 1 tr in each of next 9 ch, rep from * twice more, work [ ] twice, 1 ch, miss 1 ch, 1 tr in each of 3 (7, 11) ch to end, turn. 69 (77, 85) sts.
Beginning Grid Pattern A row 1 (7, 1) work 27 (31, 37) rows, ending Grid Pattern A row 7. 28 (32, 38) rows in all.
Shape Back Neck: First Side
next row: 2 ch, miss first tr, 1 tr in each of next 2 (6, 10) tr, [1 ch, miss 1 ch, 1 tr in each of next 3 tr] twice, 1 ch, miss 1 ch, 1 tr in each of next 9 (7, 5) tr, 2 tr tog over next 2 sts. Fasten off.
Second Side
With RS of Back facing, leave 23 (27, 31) sts at centre, join col.A to next st, 1 ch, 1 tr in next st, pattern as set to end. Fasten off.

LEFT FRONT
Grid Pattern B
row 1: 3 ch, miss first 2 tr, * 1 tr in next tr, 1 ch, miss 1 st (which may be 1 tr or 1 ch), rep from * ending 1 tr in 2nd of 2 ch at beg previous row, turn.
row 2: 2 ch, miss first tr, [1 tr in 1 ch sp, 1 tr in next tr] 1 (3, 5) times, * [1 ch, miss 1 ch, 1 tr in next tr, 1 tr in 1 ch sp, 1 tr in next tr] twice, 1 ch, miss 1 ch, [1 tr in next tr, 1 tr in 1 ch sp] 4 times, 1 tr in next tr, rep from * ending 1 tr in last tr, 1 tr in 3 ch sp, 1 tr in 2nd of 3 ch, turn.
rows 3–6: as rows 1 and 2, twice.
row 7: 2 ch, miss first tr, 1 tr in each of next 2 tr, * [1 ch, miss 1 ch, 1 tr in each of next 3 tr] twice, 1 ch, miss 1 ch, 1 tr in each of next 9 tr, rep from * ending 1 tr in each of 2 (6, 10) tr, 1 tr in 2nd of 2 ch, turn.
row 8: 2 ch, miss first tr, 1 tr in each of next 2 (6, 10) tr, * [1 ch, miss 1 ch, 1 tr in each of next 3 tr] twice, 1 ch, miss 1 ch, 1 tr in each of next 9 tr, rep from * ending 1 tr in each of 2 tr, 1 tr in 2nd of 2 ch, turn.
rows 9 and 10: as rows 7 and 8.
These 10 rows form Grid Pattern B. Repeat them as given below.
Using size 3.00 mm hook and col.A make 34 (38, 42) ch.
foundation row (RS row): 1 tr in 3rd ch from hook, 1 tr in each of next 1 (5, 9) ch, * [1 ch, miss 1 ch, 1 tr in each of next 3 ch] twice, 1 ch, miss 1 ch, 1 tr in each of next 9 ch, rep from * ending 1 tr in each of 3 ch to end, turn. 33 (37, 41) sts.
Beginning Grid Pattern B row 1 (7, 1) work 15 (17, 21) rows, ending Grid Pattern B row 3 (WS row). 16 (18, 22) rows in all.
Shape Front Neck
Keep patt constant while shaping as follows:
1st row: work in patt as set ending 2 tr tog over last ch sp and 2nd of 3 ch, turn.
2nd row: 1 ch, 1 tr in next st (= 2 tr tog), pattern as set to end, turn.
3rd row: work in patt as set ending 2 tr tog over last 2 sts, turn.
Rep 2nd and 3rd rows, 4 (5, 6) more times. 22 (24, 26) sts.
27 (31, 37) rows in all. Fasten off.

RIGHT FRONT
Grid Pattern C
row 1: 3 ch, miss first 2 tr, * 1 tr in next tr, 1 ch, miss 1 st (which may be 1 tr or 1 ch), rep from * ending 1 tr in 2nd of 2 ch at beg previous row, turn.
row 2: 2 ch, miss first tr, 1 tr in 1 ch sp, 1 tr in next tr * [1 ch, miss 1 ch, 1 tr in next tr, 1 tr in 1 ch sp, 1 tr in next tr] twice, 1 ch, miss 1 ch, [1 tr in next tr, 1 tr in 1 ch sp] 4 times, 1 tr in next tr, rep from * ending [1 tr in next tr, 1 tr in 1 ch sp] 1 (3, 5) times, 1 tr in 2nd of 3 ch, turn.
rows 3–6: as rows 1 and 2, twice.
row 7: 2 ch, miss first tr, 1 tr in each of next 2 (6, 10) tr, * [1 ch, miss 1 ch, 1 tr in each of next 3 tr] twice, 1 ch, miss 1 ch, 1 tr in each of next 9 tr, rep from * ending 1 tr in each of 2 tr, 1 tr in 2nd of 2 ch, turn.
row 8: 2 ch, miss first tr, 1 tr in each of next 2 tr, * [1 ch, miss 1 ch, 1 tr in each of next 3 tr] twice, 1 ch, miss 1 ch, 1 tr in each of next 9 tr, rep from * ending 1 tr in each of 2 (6, 10) tr, 1 tr in 2nd of 2 ch, turn.
rows 9 and 10: as rows 7 and 8.
These 10 rows form Grid Pattern C. Repeat them as given below.
Using size 3.00 mm hook and col.A make 34 (38, 42) ch.
foundation row (RS row): 1 tr in 3rd ch from hook, 1 tr in next ch, * [1 ch, miss 1 ch, 1 tr in each of next 3 ch,] twice, 1 ch, miss 1 ch,

1 tr in each of next 9 ch, rep from * ending 1 tr in each of 3 (7, 11) ch to end, turn. 33 (37, 41) sts.
Beginning Grid Pattern C row 1 (7, 1) work 15 (17, 21) rows, ending Grid Pattern C row 3 (WS row). 16 (18, 22) rows in all.

Shape Front Neck
Keep patt constant while shaping as follows:
1st row: 1 ch, 1 tr in next st (= 2 tr tog), pattern as set to end, turn.
2nd row: work in patt as set ending 2 tr tog over last 2 sts, turn.
Rep 1st and 2nd rows, 4 (5, 6) more times and 1st row once again.
22 (24, 26) sts. 27 (31, 37) rows in all. Fasten off.

SLEEVES (make 2)
Sleeves are worked from top edge down to cuff.
Using size 3.00 mm hook make 70 (78, 86) ch.
foundation row (RS row): 1 tr in 3rd ch from hook, 1 tr in each of next 1 (5, 9) ch, * [1 ch, miss 1 ch, 1 tr in each of next 3 ch] twice, 1 ch, miss 1 ch, 1 tr in each of next 9 ch, rep from * twice more, work [ ] twice, 1 ch, miss 1 ch, 1 tr in each of 3 (7, 11) ch to end, turn. 69 (77, 85) sts.
Beginning Grid Pattern A row 7 (1, 1) work 2 (4, 6) rows thus ending Grid Pattern A row 8 (4, 6).

Shape Sleeve
Keep patt constant while shaping as follows:
dec row 1: 1 ch, miss first tr, 1 tr in next st (= 2 tr tog), patt as set ending 2 tr tog over last st and 2nd ch at beg previous row, turn. 67 (75, 83) sts.
dec row 2: 1 ch, miss top of 2 tr tog, patt as set ending 2 tr tog over last 2 sts, turn. 65 (73, 81) sts.

Rep dec row 2, 14 (16, 18) more times, thus ending Grid Pattern C row 4 (2, 6). 37 (41, 45) sts. 19 (23, 27) rows in all. Work a further 4 (6, 6) rows in patt as set. 23 (29, 33) rows in all. (Adjust Sleeve length here if required.) Fasten off.

TO FINISH
Join shoulders for 22 (24, 26) sts at each side, matching patts. On each Front, count down 17 (19, 21) rows from shoulder seam and place a marker at side edge. On Back, count down 18 (20, 22) rows from shoulder seam and place a marker at each side. Join top edge of each Sleeve to armhole edge between markers, matching the mesh grids exactly.
Press as instructed on ball bands.

Weave Tartan Pattern
Lay the work on a smooth, flat surface, right side uppermost. Begin at a vertical line of holes, next to one front edge. Cut a length of col.B 4½ times longer than the line of holes. Double the thread and pass the two ends together through the needle eye. Bring needle up through lowest mesh hole and through the loop of col.B. Now thread the needle alternately up and down through the line of holes to the neck edge. Pull gently on the work to make sure the stitches are not tight, or the weaving will distort the shape. Then weave back again, filling the gaps, to the lower edge. Pass yarn to wrong side and run in the end up the wrong side of the woven line. Work towards side edge: weave next vertical line of holes in col.C, and following line in col.B. These three colours (B, C, B) are repeated for each group of three lines. Lines crossing shoulder seams should be woven as one length, from lower edge to lower edge. Weave all the lines in this direction, including the lines across the Sleeves. Join the side seams (but not the Sleeve seams), and then weave all the lines in the other direction in the same way to form the pattern. Join Sleeve seams.

TURN-BACK CUFFS (make 2)
With WS of Sleeve facing, using size 2.50 mm hook, join col.A to base of Sleeve seam.
round 1: 1 ch, 1 dc in each tr and in each 1 ch sp all round, ending 1 ss under 1 ch at beg of round.
round 2: 1 ch, 1 dc in each dc ending 1 ss under 1 ch at beg of round.
Rep round 2, 5 more times. 7 rounds in all.
edging round: Turn and with WS of cuff rounds facing: 1 ch, 1 rev. dc in each dc, ending 1 ss under 1 ch at beg of round. Fasten off.

FRONT, NECK AND LOWER EDGE BORDER
Using size 2.50 mm hook join col.A to base of right side seam.
round 1: 1 ch, 1 dc in base of each tr and 1 dc in each ch sp ending 3 dc in same place at corner, 2 dc in side edge of each row ending 2 dc tog at first neck corner, 1 dc in each st across back neck ending 2 dc tog at second neck corner, 2 dc in side edge of each row ending 3 dc in same place at second front corner, 1 dc in base of each tr and 1 dc in each ch sp around lower edge ending 1 ss under 1 ch at beg of round.
round 2: 1 ch, 1 dc in each dc, with 3 dc in same place at each

front corner and 2 dc tog at each back neck corner, ending 1 ss under 1 ch at beg of round.
round 3: as round 2, but up right front edge work: [1 dc in each of 6 (7, 9) dc, 2 ch, miss 2 ch] 4 times (complete as round 2).
round 4: as round 2, working 2 dc in each 2 ch sp.
round 5: as round 2.
edging round: Turn and with WS of border facing: 1 ch, 1 rev dc in each dc, ending 1 ss under 1 ch at beg of round. Fasten off.
Sew on buttons to match buttonholes.
Press as instructed on ball bands.

BERET

round 1: using size 3.00 mm hook and col.A, make 6 ch and join into a ring with 1 ss in first ch made.
round 2: (work over starting end) 1 ch, 12 dc into ring, 1 ss under 1 ch at beg of round. 12 sts.
round 3: 2 ch, 1 tr in st at base of these 2 ch, 2 tr in each of next 11 dc, 1 ss in 2nd of 2 ch. 24 sts.
round 4: 2 ch, 1 tr in st at base of these 2 ch, * 1 tr in next tr, [2 tr in next tr] twice, rep from * ending 1 tr in next tr, 2 tr in last tr, 1 ss in 2nd of 2 ch. 40 sts.

BERET

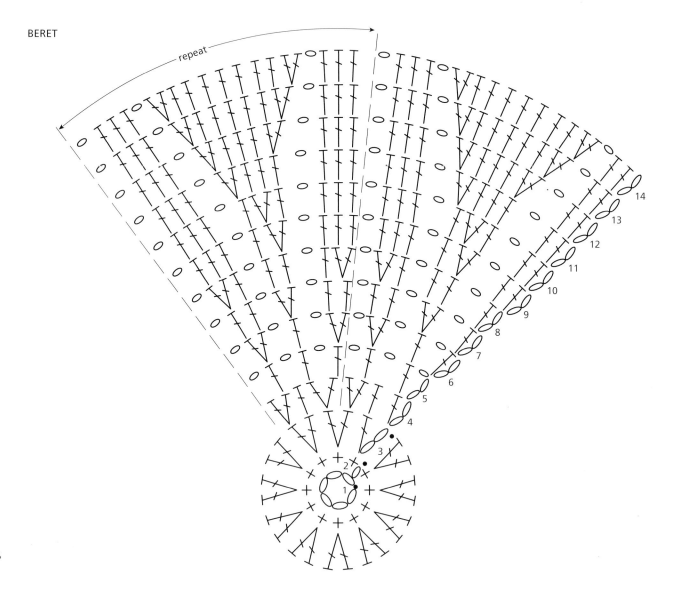

round 5: 3 ch, * [1 tr in next tr, 1 ch, miss 1 tr] twice, 1 tr in next tr, 1 ch, rep from * ending 1 ss in 2nd of 3 ch. 48 sts.

round 6: 2 ch, 1 tr in st at base of these 2 ch, 1 ch, miss 1 ch, * 1 tr in next tr, 1 ch, miss 1 ch, [2 tr in next tr, 1 ch, miss 1 ch] twice, rep from * ending 2 tr in last tr, 1 ch, 1 ss in 2nd of 3 ch. 64 sts.

round 7: 2 ch, 1 tr in next tr, * 1 ch, miss 1 ch, 2 tr in next tr, [1 ch, miss 1 ch, 1 tr in each of next 2 trs] twice, rep from * ending 1 ss in 2nd of 3 ch. 72 sts.

round 8: 2 ch, 1 tr in st at base of these 2 ch, 1 tr in next tr, * 1 ch, miss 1 ch, 1 tr in each of next 2 tr, 1 ch, miss 1 ch, 1 tr in first of 2 tr, 2 tr in next tr, 1 ch, miss 1 ch, 2 tr in first of 2 tr, 1 tr in next tr, rep from * ending 1 ch, 1 ss in 2nd of 2 ch. 88 sts. (Check tension here.)

round 9: 2 ch, 1 tr in each of next 2 tr, * 1 ch, miss 1 ch, 2 tr in first of 2 tr, 1 tr in next tr, [1 ch, miss 1 ch, 1 tr in each of next 3 tr] twice, rep from * ending 1 ch, 1 ss in 2nd of 2 ch. 96 sts.

round 10: 2 ch, 1 tr in each of 2 tr, * 1 ch, miss 1 ch, 1 tr in next tr, 2 tr in next tr, 1 tr in next tr, [1 ch, miss 1 ch, 1 tr in each of next 3 tr] twice, rep from * ending 1 ch, 1 ss in 2nd of 2 ch. 104 sts.

round 11: 2 ch, 1 tr in each of next 2 tr, * 1 ch, miss 1 ch, 1 tr in each of next 3 tr, 2 tr in next tr, [1 ch, miss 1 ch, 1 tr in each of next 3 tr] twice, rep from * ending 1 ch, 1 ss in 2nd of 2 ch. 112 sts.

round 12: 2 ch, 1 tr in each of next 2 tr, * 1 ch, miss 1 ch, 2 tr in first of 5 tr, 1 tr in each of next 3 tr, 2 tr in next tr, [1 ch, miss 1 ch, 1 tr in each of next 3 tr] twice, rep from * ending 1 ss in 2nd of 2 ch. 128 sts.

2nd and 3rd Sizes Only

round 13: 2 ch, 1 tr in each of next 2 tr, * 1 ch, miss 1 ch, 2 tr in first of 7 tr, 1 tr in each of 5 tr, 2 tr in next tr, [1 ch, miss 1 ch, 1 tr in each of next 3 tr] twice, rep from * ending 1 ss in 2nd of 2 ch. 144 sts.

3rd Size Only

round 14: 2 ch, 1 tr in each of next 2 tr, * 1 ch, miss 1 ch, 2 tr in first of 9 tr, 1 tr in each of 7 tr, 2 tr in next tr, [1 ch, miss 1 ch, 1 tr in each of next 3 tr] twice, rep from * ending 1 ss in 2nd of 2 ch. 160 sts.

All Sizes

128 (144, 160) sts.

mesh round: 3 ch, miss 1 st (which may be 1 ch or 1 tr), 1 tr in next tr, * 1 ch, miss 1 st, 1 tr in next tr, rep from * ending 1 ch, miss 1 st, 1 ss in 2nd of 3 ch.

foll round: 2 ch, 1 tr in 1 ch sp, 1 tr in next tr, * 1 ch, miss 1 ch, [1 tr in next tr, 1 tr in 1 ch sp] 3 (4, 5) times, 1 tr in next tr, [1 ch, miss 1 ch, 1 tr in next tr, 1 tr in 1 ch sp, 1 tr in next tr] twice, rep from * ending 1 ch, miss 1 ch, 1 ss in 2nd of 2 ch.
Rep mesh round and foll round twice more.

2nd and 3rd Sizes Only

next round: 2 ch, 1 tr in each tr and [1 ch, miss 1 ch] over each 1 ch sp, ending 1 ss in 2nd of 2 ch.

3rd Size Only

Rep last round once more.

All Sizes

18 (20, 22) rounds in all.

dec round: 2 ch, 2 tr tog over next 2 tr, * 1 ch, miss 1 ch, 1 tr in next tr, [2 tr tog over next 2 tr] 3 (4, 5) times, [1 ch, miss 1 ch, 1 tr in next tr, 2 tr tog over next 2 tr] twice, ending 1 ch, miss 1 ch, 1 ss in 2nd of 2 ch. 88 (96, 104) sts.

Border

Change to size 2.50 mm hook.

1st round: 1 ch, 1 dc in each st (including ch sps), ending 1 ss under 1 ch at beg of round.

2nd round: 1 ch, 1 dc in each dc, ending 1 ss under 1 ch at beg of round.
Rep 2nd round 5 more times.

edging round: Turn and with WS of border facing: 1 ch, 1 rev dc in each dc, ending 1 ss under 1 ch at beg of round. Fasten off.

TO FINISH

Pull gently on starting end of yarn to tighten centre of Beret.
Use cols.B and C to weave the pattern in the same way as the Jacket, beginning at round 4 at the centre of the beret and ending at the border.
Use col.C to make a tassel: wind yarn about 20 times round a piece of card 10 cm (4 in) wide. Pass a length of yarn under the threads at one edge of card and tie firmly leaving ends at least 20 cm (8 in) long. Cut through the threads at the other edge of the card (diagram 1). Tie firmly with another length of yarn, about 1.5 cm (½ in) from top (diagram 2). Use the long ends to sew the tassel to the centre of the Beret.

diagram 1   diagram 2

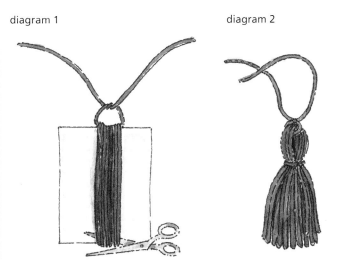

TWO-COLOUR JUMPER

BOLD, BRIGHT AND FUN TO WORK USING THE TECHNIQUE OF TWO-COLOUR ROWS.

SIZES

to fit chest	56	61	66 cm
	22	24	26 in
actual measurement	61	66	71 cm
	24	26	28 in
length to shoulder	35	39	45 cm
	13¾	15¼	17¾ in
sleeve seam with cuff	24	28	33 cm
folded back	9½	11	13 in

MATERIALS

3 (4, 5) x 50 g balls of Sirdar Country Style DK
in col.A (414 Ivory Cream)
1 (1, 1) x 50 g ball of Sirdar Country Style DK
in col.B (426 Cerise)
4.00 mm and 4.50 mm hooks
2 buttons
stitch holder

TENSION
15½ sts and 10 rows to 10 cm (4 in) measured over Two-Colour Pattern using size 4.50 mm hook.

NOTE
Carry col.B loosely up side edge of work between two-colour rows – no need to fasten off.

BACK
Using size 4.50 mm hook and col.A make 48 (52, 56) ch.
foundation row: 1 dc in 2nd ch from hook, 1 dc in each ch to end, 1 ch, turn. 47 (51, 55) dc.
Two-Colour Pattern
row 1 (WS row): using col.A, 2 ch (do not count as first st), 1 htr in first st, 1 htr in each st to end, turn.
row 2: using col.A, 2 ch, 1 htr in first htr, 1 htr in each st to end, turn.
row 3 (WS row): change to col.B, 1 ch, 1 dc in first htr, * 1 ch, miss 1 htr, 1 dc in next htr, rep from * to end, leave working lp on holder. Without turning work insert hook in first dc of B at beg of row, pull through a lp of A, 1 ch, 1 dc in same dc of B, * 1 tr in htr of A below first ch sp (enclosing ch of B), 1 dc in next dc of B, rep from * to end, 1 ss in lp of B on holder, turn. Remove holder.
row 4: as row 1.
row 5: as row 2.
row 6 (RS row): change to col.B, 1 ss in first htr, 3 ch, miss next htr,

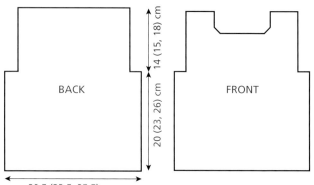

BACK

FRONT

14 (15, 18) cm

20 (23, 26) cm

30.5 (33.5, 35.5) cm

27.5 (30.5, 33) cm

4 cm

SLEEVE

23 (27.5, 32) cm

18.5 (20, 21.5) cm

TWO COLOUR PATTERN

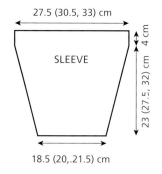
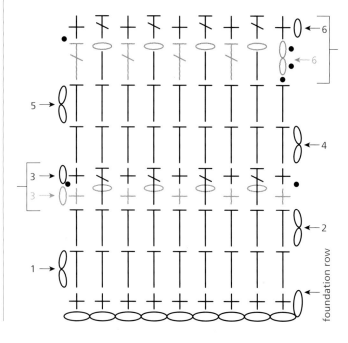

foundation row

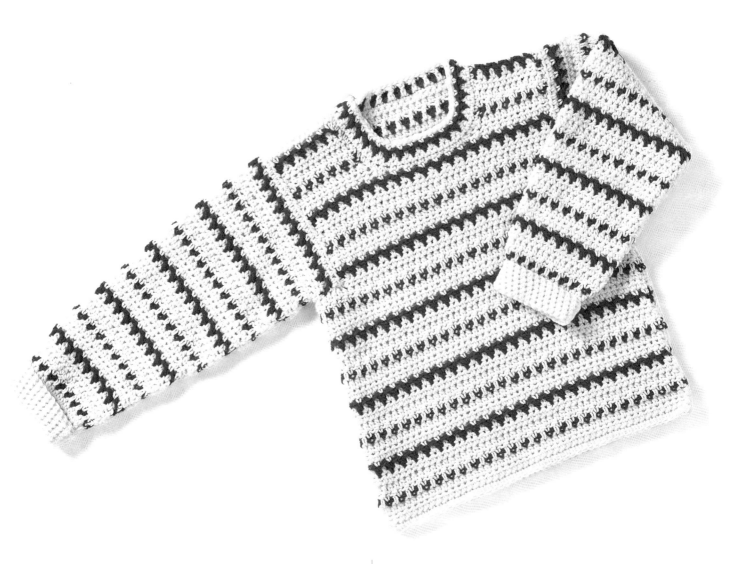

* 1 tr in next htr, 1 ch, miss 1 htr, rep from * ending 1 tr in last htr, leave working lp on holder. Without turning work insert hook in first ch of B at beg of row, pull through a lp of A, 1 ss in next ch of B, 1 ch, 1 dc in same ch of B as 1 ss, * 1 tr behind ch of B into htr of A below, 1 dc in next tr of B, rep from * to end, 1 ss in lp of B on holder, turn. Remove holder.

These 6 rows form the Two-Colour Pattern. Rep them 2 (2, 3) more times. 19 (19, 25) rows in all.

Work patt rows 1 (1–4, 1) again. 20 (23, 26) rows in all. Fasten off both cols.

Shape Armholes
With RS (WS, RS) of work facing, rejoin col.A to 7th htr of last row.
next row: 2 ch, 1 htr in same htr, 1 htr in each of next 34 (38, 42) htr, turn leaving last 6 htr unworked. 35 (39, 43) htr. **
Beg patt row 3 (6, 3) work 13 (14, 17) more patt rows thus ending patt row 3 (1, 1). Fasten off.

FRONT
Work as Back to **.
Beg patt row 3 (6, 3) work 7 (7, 10) more patt rows thus ending patt row 3 (6, 6).

Shape Neck: First Side
1st row: using A, 2 ch, 1 htr in first st, 1 htr in each of next 8 (10, 10) sts, 2 htr tog over next 2 sts, turn. 10 (12, 12) sts.
2nd row: 2 ch, 2 htr tog over 2 htr tog and next htr, 1 htr in each htr to end, turn. 9 (11, 11) sts.

Beg patt row 6 (3, 3) work 4 (5, 5) more rows thus ending patt row 3 (1, 1). Fasten off.

Second Side
With RS (WS, WS) of work facing, leave 12 (12, 16) sts at centre front, rejoin col.A to next st.
1st row: 2 ch, 2 htr tog over next 2 sts, 1 htr in each st to end, turn. 10 (12, 12) sts.
2nd row: 2 ch, 1 htr in first htr, 1 htr in each of next 7 (9, 9) htr, 2 htr tog over last htr and 2 htr tog, turn. 9 (11, 11) sts.
Beg patt row 6 (3, 3) work 4 (5, 5) more rows thus ending patt row 3 (1, 1). Fasten off.

SLEEVES (make 2)
Using size 4.50 mm hook and col.A make 30 (32, 34) ch.
Work foundation row as for Back. 29 (31, 33) dc.

Shape Sleeve
inc row 1: using A, 2 ch, 2 htr in first st, 1 htr in each st to end, turn.
inc row 2: using A, 2 ch, 2 htr in first htr, 1 htr in each htr to end, turn.
inc row 3: as Two-Colour Pattern row 3.
inc rows 4 and 5: as inc rows 1 and 2.
inc row 6: as Two-Colour Pattern row 6. 33 (35, 37) sts.
Rep these 6 rows 2 (3, 3) more times.

1st and 3rd Sizes Only
Work inc rows 1 and 2 once again.

All Sizes

43 (47, 51) sts. 21 (25, 27) rows in all ending inc row 2 (6, 2).
Beg patt row 3 (1, 3) work in Two-Colour Pattern until Sleeve measures 23 (27, 32) cm (9 [10½, 12½] in) in all.
Place a marker at each end of last row. Work 4 more patt rows. Fasten off.

NECKBAND

Join left shoulder seam. With RS of work facing, using size 4.00 mm hook join col.A at armhole edge of right shoulder on Back.

row 1: 1 ch, 1 dc in first st, 1 dc in each st along top of Back to shoulder seam, 2 dc tog at corner, 10 (12, 12) dc down side edge of first side of front neck shaping, 2 dc tog at corner, 1 dc in each st along centre front, 2 dc tog at corner, 10 (12, 12) dc up side edge of front neck shaping to corner, turn.

row 2: 1 ch, 1 dc in first dc, 1 dc in each dc to last 9 (11, 11) dc, turn, leaving last 9 (11, 11) dc to form edging of Back shoulder. (Count number of dc on this row: there should be an odd number, if not work 2 dc tog at centre back.)

row 3: change to col.B, 1 ss in first dc, 3 ch, miss next dc, * 1 tr in next dc, 1 ch, miss 1 dc, rep from * ending 1 tr in last dc, leave working lp on holder. Without turning work insert hook in first ch of B at beg of row, pull through a lp of A, 1 ss in next ch of B, 1 ch, 1 dc in same ch of B as 1 ss, * 1 tr behind ch of B into dc of A below, 1 dc in next tr of B, rep from * to end, 1 ss in lp of B from holder, turn. Remove holder.

row 4: 1 ch, 1 ss in each st to end. Fasten off.

BUTTONHOLE BAND

With RS of work facing using size 4.00 mm hook join col.A to corner of Neckband at left front shoulder.

row 1: 1 ch, 5 dc in side edge of Neckband, 1 dc in each of 9 (11, 11) htr along shoulder edge, turn. 14(16, 16) dc.

row 2: 1 ch, 1 dc in first dc, 1 dc in each of next 2 dc, [2 ch, miss 2 dc, 1 dc in each of next 2 (3, 3) dc] twice, 2 ch, miss 2 dc, 1 dc in last dc, turn.

row 3: 1 ch, 1 dc in first dc, 2 dc in each ch sp and 1 dc in each dc to end. Fasten off.

TO FINISH

Lap Buttonhole Band over Back, matching edges of last rows of Back and Front, and sew down side edge of Buttonhole Band at armhole edge.
Join top edges of Sleeves to armhole edges, with Sleeve rows above markers matching armhole shapings.
Join side and sleeve seams, matching patt rows.

Cuffs (make 2)

With RS of Sleeve facing, using size 4.00 mm hook join col.A at base of sleeve seam.

round 1: 1 ch, 1 dc in base of each of 29 (31, 33) ch, 1 ss in first dc of round.

round 2: 1 ch, 1 dc in each of first 3 (3, 4) dc, [2 dc tog over next 2 dc, 1 dc in each of next 3 (4, 4) dc] 4 times, 2 dc tog over next 2 dc, 1 dc in each dc ending 1 dc in first dc of round. 5 decs made.

round 3: 1 dc in each dc, ending 1 dc in first dc of round.
Rep round 3, 6 more times. Fasten off.

Lower Edge

With RS of work facing, using size 4.00 mm hook join col.A at base of one side seam in sp between 2 dc of first row.

round 1: 1 ch, 1 dc in same sp, 1 dc in each sp between 2 dc of first row all round, ending 1 ss in first dc of round. Fasten off.
Sew on buttons to match buttonholes.
Press as instructed on ball bands.

TWO HATS

ONE BASIC PATTERN MAKES TWO DESIGNS: ADD EARS, FACE
AND TAIL FOR A FRIENDLY RABBIT, OR ADD THE STALK AND
FRUIT TRIM.

SIZES

to fit head	45.5	48	50.5 cm
	18	19	20 in

MAIN SHAPE

19 (20, 21.5) cm

46 (48.5, 51) cm

EAR

12.5 cm

12.5 cm

MATERIALS

RABBIT HAT
2 (2, 2) x 50 g balls of Jaeger Matchmaker Merino 4-ply in
col.A (782 Flannel)
oddments of black and white DK or 4-ply wool
3.00 mm hook
15 x 15 cm (6 x 6 in) polyester wadding
blunt-ended tapestry needle for embroidery
darning needle
thin card
FRUIT HAT
1 (2, 2) x 50 g balls of Jaeger Matchmaker Merino 4-ply in
col.A (715 Thyme)
small ball of Jaeger Matchmaker Merino 4-ply in
col.B (713 Meadow)
oddment of Jaeger Matchmaker Merino 4-ply in
col.C (697 Peony)
3.00 mm hook

TENSION
First 13 rounds should measure 10 cm (4 in) in diameter.

RABBIT HAT

MAIN SHAPE
round 1: using size 3.00 mm hook and col.A, make 6 ch and join
into a ring with 1 ss in first ch made.
round 2: (work over starting end): 1 ch, 12 dc into ring, 1 ss in first
dc of round. 12 sts.
round 3: 1 ch, 1 dc in st at base of this ch, [1 dc in next dc, 2 dc in
next dc] 5 times, 1 dc in next dc, 1 ss in 1 ch at beg of round. 18 sts.
round 4: 1 ch, 1 dc in st at base of this ch, [1 dc in each of next
2 dc, 2 dc in next dc] 5 times, 1 dc in each of next 2 dc, 1 ss in 1 ch
at beg of round. 24 sts.
round 5: 1 ch, 1 dc in st at base of this ch, [1 dc in each of next
3 dc, 2 dc in next dc] 5 times, 1 dc in each of next 3 dc, 1 ss in 1 ch
at beg of round. 30 sts.
round 6: 1 ch, 1 dc in st at base of this ch, [1 dc in each of next
4 dc, 2 dc in next dc] 5 times, 1 dc in each of next 4 dc, 1 ss in 1 ch
at beg of round. 36 sts.
round 7: 1 ch, 1 dc in st at base of this ch, [1 dc in each of next
5 dc, 2 dc in next dc] 5 times, 1 dc in each of next 5 dc, 1 ss in 1 ch
at beg of round. 42 sts.
round 8: 1 ch, 1 dc in st at base of this ch, [1 dc in each of next
6 dc, 2 dc in next dc] 5 times, 1 dc in each of next 6 dc, 1 ss in 1 ch
at beg of round. 48 sts.
round 9: 1 ch, 1 dc in st at base of this ch, [1 dc in each of next
7 dc, 2 dc in next dc] 5 times, 1 dc in each of next 7 dc, 1 ss in 1 ch

ROUNDS 1-5

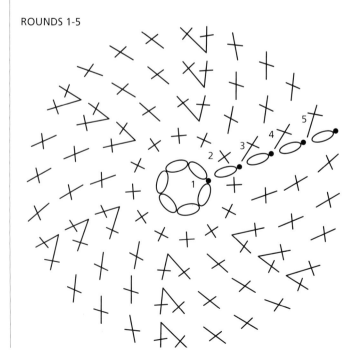

at beg of round. 54 sts.

round 10: 1 ch, 1 dc in st at base of this ch, [1 dc in each of next 8 dc, 2 dc in next dc] 5 times, 1 dc in each of next 8 dc, 1 ss in 1 ch at beg of round. 60 sts.

round 11: 1 ch, 1 dc in st at base of this ch, [1 dc in each of next 9 dc, 2 dc in next dc] 5 times, 1 dc in each of next 9 dc, 1 ss in 1 ch at beg of round. 66 sts.

round 12: 1 ch, 1 dc in st at base of this ch, [1 dc in each of next 10 dc, 2 dc in next dc] 5 times, 1 dc in each of next 10 dc, 1 ss in 1 ch at beg of round. 72 sts.

round 13: 1 ch, 1 dc in st at base of this ch, [1 dc in each of next 11 dc, 2 dc in next dc] 5 times, 1 dc in each of next 11 dc, 1 ss in 1 ch at beg of round. 78 sts. (Check tension here.)

round 14: 1 ch, 1 dc in st at base of this ch, [1 dc in each of next 12 dc, 2 dc in next dc] 5 times, 1 dc in each of next 12 dc, 1 ss in 1 ch at beg of round. 84 sts.

round 15: 1 ch, 1 dc in st at base of this ch, [1 dc in each of next 13 dc, 2 dc in next dc] 5 times, 1 dc in each of next 13 dc, 1 ss in 1 ch at beg of round. 90 sts.

round 16: 1 ch, 1 dc in st at base of this ch, [1 dc in each of next 14 dc, 2 dc in next dc] 5 times, 1 dc in each of next 14 dc, 1 ss in 1 ch at beg of round. 96 sts.

round 17: 1 ch, 1 dc in st at base of this ch, [1 dc in each of next 15 dc, 2 dc in next dc] 5 times, 1 dc in each of next 15 dc, 1 ss in 1 ch at beg of round. 102 sts.

2nd and 3rd Sizes Only

round 18: 1 ch, 1 dc in st at base of this ch, [1 dc in each of next 16 dc, 2 dc in next dc] 5 times, 1 dc in each of next 16 dc, 1 ss in 1 ch at beg of round. 108 sts.

3rd Size Only

round 19: 1 ch, 1 dc in st at base of this ch, [1 dc in each of next 17 dc, 2 dc in next dc] 5 times, 1 dc in each of next 17 dc, 1 ss in 1 ch at beg of round. 114 sts.

diagram 1

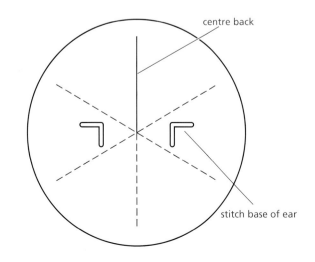

centre back

stitch base of ear

diagram 2

All Sizes

102 (108, 114) sts.

plain round: 1 ch, 1 dc in st at base of this ch, 1 dc in each dc to last dc, miss last dc, 1 ss in 1 ch at beg of round.

Rep this round until Hat measures 15 (16.5, 18) cm (6 [6½, 7] in) from centre to outside edge ending with a complete round.

dec round: 1 ch, miss 1 dc at base of this ch, [1 dc in each of next 15 (16, 17) dc, 2 dc tog over next 2 dc] 5 times, 1 dc in each of next 15 (16, 17) dc, 1 ss in 1 ch at beg of round. 96 (102, 108) sts.

Rep plain round until Hat measures 19 (20, 21.5) cm (7½ [8, 8½] in) from centre to outside edge, ending with a complete round. Fasten off.

Allow lower edge to roll towards right side of work.

EARS (make 2)

round 1: using size 3.00 mm hook and col.A, make 30 ch and join into a ring with 1 ss in first ch made.

round 2: 1 ch, 1 dc in ch at base of this ch, 1 dc in each ch to last ch, miss last ch, 1 ss in 1 ch at beg of round. 30 sts.

round 3: 1 ch, 1 dc in st at base of this ch, 1 dc in each dc to last dc, miss last dc, 1 ss in 1 ch at beg of round.

Rep round 3, 15 more times. 18 rounds.

dec round: 1 ch, miss st at base of this ch, 1 dc in each dc to last 3 dc, 2 dc tog over next 2 dc, miss last dc, 1 ss in 1 ch at beg of round. 28 sts.

foll round: 1 ch, 1 dc in st at base of this ch, 1 dc in each dc to 2 dc tog, miss this last st, 1 ss in 1 ch at beg of round.

diagram 3

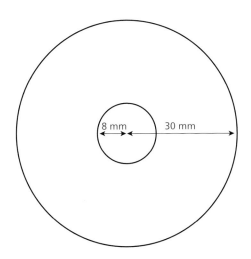

8 mm   30 mm

Rep these 2 rounds twice more. 24 sts.
Rep dec round 9 more times. 6 sts. Fasten off.

TO FINISH

Press ears flat with shaping at centre front. Cut a piece of wadding to same shape as each ear, slip inside ears. Use col.A and darning needle to work a line of chain st (as page 12) down the centre of each ear to cover the shaping line, catching down to the wadding but not through to the back of the ear. Slip stitch along the base of each ear to enclose the wadding. Fold the base to form a right angle and sew to top of hat as indicated on diagram 1. (You may find it helpful to stretch the hat over a bowl or child's ball.)

Use black yarn to embroider features as shown on diagram 2.

Use compasses to draw diagram 3 twice on thin card. Use white yarn to make a pompom as given on page 108 (Nursery Cushion). Sew pompom at centre back.

FRUIT HAT

Using col.A work Main Shape as for Rabbit Hat.

FRUIT TRIM
Fruit Chain
Using size 3.00 mm hook and col.C make 9 ch.
round 1: 7 dtr tog in 4th ch from hook, [9 ch, 7 dtr tog in 4th ch from hook] twice, join into a ring with 1 ss in first ch made.
Fasten off.
Stalk
Using size 3.00 mm hook and col.B make 10 ch.
row 1: 1 dc in 2nd ch from hook, 1 dc in each of next 8 ch, turn. 9 dc.
row 2: 1 ch, 1 dc in first dc, 1 dc in each dc to end, turn.
Rep row 2, 4 more times. 6 rows.
next row: fold lower edge up to meet top edge and work through both thicknesses to form a tube: 1 ch, [1 ss through both thicknesses] 9 times.
Continue in rounds:
round 1: 1 ch, 6 dc evenly spaced around end of tube (inserting hook from outside of tube through to inside), ending 1 ss in first dc of round.
round 2: 1 ch, 1 dc in dc at base of this ch, 2 dc in each of next 5 dc, 1 ss in 1 ch at beg of round. 12 sts.
round 3: 1 ch, 1 dc in dc at base of this ch, [1 dc in next dc, 2 dc in next dc] 5 times, 1 dc in last dc, 1 ss in 1 ch at

beg of round. 18 sts.
Slip Fruit Chain over Stalk.
round 4: 1 ch, 1 dc in dc at base of this ch tog with first ch sp of Fruit Chain, [1 dc in each of next 2 dc, 2 dc in next dc, 1 dc in each of next 2 dc] all tog with same ch sp of Fruit Chain, * push fruit bobble to RS of work, [2 dc in next dc, 1 dc in each of next 2 dc] tog with next ch sp of Fruit Chain, twice; rep from * once more, push fruit bobble to RS of work, 1 ss in 1 ch at beg of round. 24 sts.
First Leaf
row 1: 1 ch, 1 dc in dc at base of this ch, 1 dc in each of next 2 dc, 2 dc in next dc, turn. 5 dc.
row 2: 1 ch, 1 dc in each of first 4 dc, 2 dc in last dc, turn. 6 dc.
row 3: 1 ch, 1 dc in first dc, 1 dc in each dc to end, turn.
Rep row 3, 7 more times. 10 rows.
row 11: 1 ch, miss first dc, 1 dc in each dc to end, turn. 5 dc.
Rep row 11, 3 more times. 2 dc.
row 15: 1 ch, miss first dc, 1 dc in last dc. 1 st. Fasten off.
Second Leaf
With RS of trim facing rejoin col.B to next dc of round 4. Work as First Leaf.
Work 4 more leaves in the same way, without fastening off last leaf.
edging round: 1 ch, * 1 dc in side edge of each row of leaf, 3 dc tog at inner corner, 1 dc in side edge of each row of next leaf, 4 dc in same place at outer point, rep from * all round edge of trim ending 1 ss in 1 ch at beg of round. Fasten off.
Sew Fruit Trim to centre top of hat, spreading the leaves evenly. Use col.B to backstitch all round the edge of the trim.

CHRISTENING SHAWL

WARM, LIGHT AND SMOOTH TO THE TOUCH, PURE SILK YARN MAKES THIS SHAWL A FAMILY HEIRLOOM.

SIZE

approx. 110 x 110 cm (43 x 43 in)

MATERIALS

2 x 150 g cones of undyed Texere Yarns 2-ply silk yarn (ref.SS16)
2.50 mm hook

TENSION

Work Centre Square ending round 4. Press as instructed on yarn band. Square should measure 5.5 cm (2¼ in) in each direction. If your square is too small, try again with a larger hook; if it is too large, try a smaller hook.
Tension is not crucial provided a change in finished size is acceptable. However, if your tension is too tight, the shawl may feel too firm, and if your tension is too loose, the shawl may not hold its shape and extra yarn may be required.

Special Abbreviations: 3 tr tog: [yrh, insert in sp as given, yrh, pull through a lp, yrh, pull through 2 lps] three times, yrh, pull through 4 lps on hook.
2 dtr tog: *yrh twice, insert in sp as given, yrh, pull through a lp, [yrh, pull through 2 lps] twice, rep from * once more, yrh, pull through 3 lps on hook.
3 dtr tog: *yrh twice, insert in sp as given, yrh, pull through a lp, [yrh, pull through 2 lps] twice, rep from * twice more, yrh, pull through 4 lps on hook.
1 fan: 1 dtr, 4 tr in base lp of this d tr, inserting hook behind 2 threads.

This design is worked in rounds, beginning at centre of shawl:

CENTRE SQUARE

Using size 2.50 mm hook, make 6 ch and join into a ring with 1 ss in first ch made.
round 1: 1 ch, 12 dc into ring and over starting end of yarn, 1 ss under 1 ch at beg of round.
round 2: 3 ch, 1 tr in same place as base of 3 ch, 2 tr in each of rem 11 dc, ending 1 ss in 3rd of 3 ch at beg of round. 24 sts.
round 3: 3 ch, 2 dtr tog inserting hook in each of next 2 trs, * 3 ch, [3 tr tog inserting hook in same place as last st and in each of next 2 trs, 3 ch] twice, 3 dtr tog inserting hook in same place as last st and in each of next 2 trs, rep from * twice more, 3 ch, 3 tr tog inserting hook as before, 3 ch, 3 tr tog inserting hook in same place

as last st, in next tr and in st at base of 3 ch at beg of round, 3 ch, 1 ss in top of 2 dtr tog.

round 4: 4 ch, 1 ss in top of 2 dtr tog at base of ch (first picot made), * 3 dc in 3 ch sp, 1 dc in top of next group, 3 ch, 1 ss in same place as last dc (second picot made), rep from * ending 1 ss in first of 4 ch at beg of round. (Check your tension here.)

round 5: 1 dc in corner picot, * 5 ch, 1 dc in same corner picot, 5 ch, 1 dc in next picot, 3 ch, 1 dc in next picot, 5 ch, 1 dc in next corner picot, rep from * ending 1 ss in dc at beg of round.

round 6: [1 dc, 3 ch, 1 fan] in corner ch sp, * 5 tr in 3rd of next 5 ch, 5 tr in 2nd of next 3 ch, 5 tr in 3rd of next 5 ch, 2 fans in corner ch sp, rep from * ending 4 tr in 1 dc at beg of round, 1 ss in 3rd of 3 ch.

FAN PATTERN

round 7: [1 dc, 3 ch, 1 fan] in corner sp before next fan, * miss 1 fan, [1 fan in sp before next 5 tr, miss 5 tr] 3 times, 1 fan in sp before next fan, miss 1 fan, 2 fans in corner sp, rep from * ending 4 tr in 1 dc at beg of round, 1 ss in 3rd of 3 ch. 6 fans on each side of square.

round 8: [1 dc, 3 ch, 1 fan] in sp before next fan, * [miss 1 fan, 1 fan in sp before next fan] to corner, 2 fans in corner sp, rep from * ending 4 tr in 1 dc at beg of round, 1 ss in 3rd of 3 ch. 7 fans on each side of square.

CENTRE SQUARE rounds 1-7

FAN MESH PATTERN

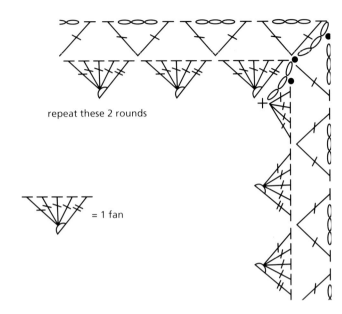

repeat these 2 rounds

= 1 fan

Rep round 8, 17 more times. 24 fans on each side of square. Fasten off.

FIRST BAND OF SQUARES
First Square
Work as Centre Square rounds 1–3.
round 4: as round 4 of Centre Square, but joining 3rd side to last round of Fan Pattern as follows: (hold both pieces with right sides uppermost) at 3rd corner, instead of 3 ch picot, work [1 ch, 1 ss between 2 corner fans inserting hook from WS through to RS, 1 ch], * instead of next 3 ch picot, work [1 ch, 1 ss between next 2 fans along side edge inserting hook as before, 1 ch], rep from * once, work 4th corner as 3rd, then complete the round as set ending 1 ss in first of 4 ch. Fasten off.

Second Square
Work as First Square, but join 2nd corner to 1st corner of previous square, 2nd side to 4th side of previous square, 3rd corner to same sp as 4th corner of previous square and 3rd side to last row of Fan Pattern, working clockwise round the edge of the main piece. Work a further 34 squares in the same way, joining them as shown on general layout diagram. Note that corner squares will be joined to two squares along two adjacent sides and to centre section at one corner only.

FAN MESH PATTERN
1st round: With right side of work facing, rejoin yarn to picot at one corner, 4 ch, 1 ss in same picot, * 5 ch, 1 dc in next picot, 3 ch,

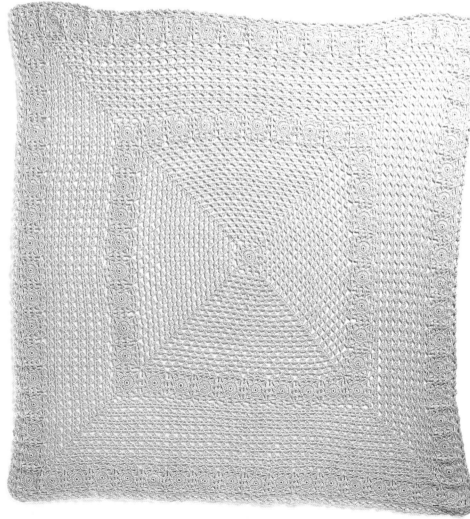

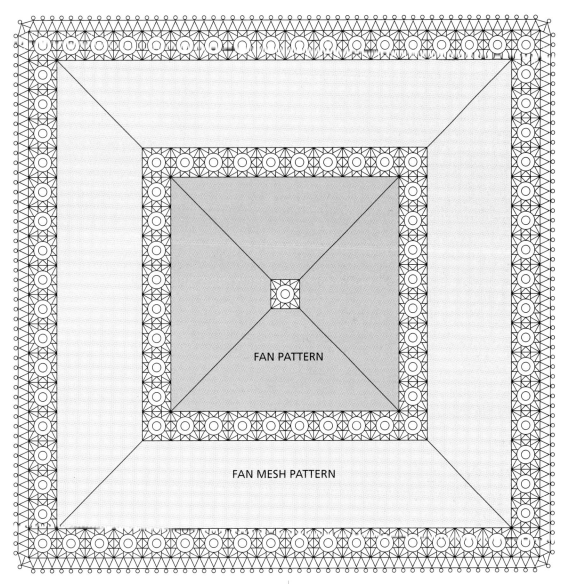

FAN PATTERN

FAN MESH PATTERN

1 dc in next picot, 5 ch, 2 dc tog over 2 joined picots, [[rep from * ending [1 dc, 3 ch, 1 dc] in corner picot]] 3 times, rep from * along 4th side ending 1 ss in first of 4 ch at beg of round.

2nd round: [1 dc, 3 ch, 1 fan] in corner sp before next fan, * miss 1 fan, [1 fan in sp before next 5 tr, miss 5 tr] 3 times, 1 fan in sp before next fan, miss 1 fan, 2 fans in corner sp, rep from * ending 4 tr in 1 dc at beg of round, 1 ss in 3rd of 3 ch.

3rd round: 3 ch, [1 tr, 3 ch, 1 tr] in corner sp, * miss 5 tr, [1 tr, 3 ch, 1 tr] in sp before next 5 tr, [[rep from * ending [1 tr, 3 ch, 1 tr] twice in corner sp]] 3 times, rep from * along 4th side ending 1 tr in first corner sp, 3 ch, 1 ss in 3rd of 3 ch at beg of round.

4th round: 1 dc in sp before next tr, 3 ch, 1 fan in same corner sp, * miss [1 tr, 3 ch, 1 tr], 1 fan in sp before next group, [rep from * ending 2 fans in corner sp] 3 times, rep from * along 4th side ending 4 tr in dc at beg of round, 1 ss in 3rd of 3 ch.

5th round: 1 ss in corner sp, 3 ch, [1 tr, 3 ch, 1 tr] in same corner sp, * miss 1 fan, [1 tr, 3 ch, 1 tr] in sp before next fan, [[rep from * ending [1 tr, 3 ch, 1 tr] in corner sp]] 3 times, rep from * along 4th side ending 1 tr in first corner sp, 3 ch, 1 ss in 3rd of 3 ch at beg of round.

Rep 4th and 5th rounds, 6 more times, and 4th round once again. 48 fans on each side of square.

SECOND BAND OF SQUARES
Work as First Band of Squares, making 68 squares in all.

BORDER
With right side of shawl facing, rejoin yarn to one corner picot.
border round 1: as 1st round of Fan Mesh Pattern.
border round 2: [1 dc, 3 ch, 1 dc] in corner ch sp, miss 1 dc, *[5 dc in 5 ch sp, 1 dc in next dc, 3 dc in 3 ch sp, 1 dc in dc, 5 dc in 5 ch sp, miss 2 dc tog] to next corner, ending miss 1 dc, [1 dc, 3 ch, 1 dc] in corner ch sp, rep from * 3 more times, ending miss 1 dc, 1 ss in first dc of round.

border round 3: 3 ch, 4 tr tog (working first 3 sts in corner ch sp and 4th st in next dc), 3 ch, 1 ss in top of last 4 tr tog, 4 ch, * [5 tr tog over next 5 dc, 3 ch, 1 ss in top of last 5 tr tog, 4 ch] to next corner ending 5 tr tog (working first st in next dc, next 3 sts in corner ch sp and 5th st in next dc), 3 ch, 1 ss in top of last 5 tr tog, 4 ch, rep from * 3 more times ending 1 ss in top of 4 tr tog at beg of round.

border round 4: 1 dc in corner picot, * 3 dc in same picot, 2 dc tog over same picot and next ch sp, 2 dc in same ch sp, 2 dc tog over same ch sp and next picot, rep from * ending 1 ss in first dc of round. Fasten off.
Press as instructed on yarn label.

91

GIRAFFE AND ZEBRA

CUDDLY TOYS TO MAKE WITH ODD BALLS OF YARN.

SIZES

GIRAFFE	approx. height	31 cm (12¼ in)
ZEBRA	approx. height	22 cm (8½ in)

MATERIALS

GIRAFFE
1 x 100 g ball of Patons Knit 'n Save DK in col.A (7730 Melon)
oddment of Patons Knit 'n Save DK in col.B (7814 Black)
3.50 mm hook
toy filling
ZEBRA
1 x 100 g ball of Patons Knit 'n Save DK in col.A (7814 Black)
1 x 100 g ball of Patons Knit 'n Save DK in col.B (7813 Snow White)
oddment of Patons Knit 'n Save DK in col.C (7796 Orange)
3.50 mm hook
toy filling

TENSION

20 sts and 20 rows to 10 cm (4 in) measured over rows of double crochet using size 3.50 mm hook.
Tension is not crucial provided a change in size is acceptable. However, if your tension is too loose the toy will not hold its shape.

NOTE

Instructions are for DK yarn, but you can use a finer or heavier yarn if you wish, changing the hook size accordingly. The crochet fabric should be firm. (Changing the yarn and hook will alter the finished size.)

GIRAFFE

SIDE OF BODY (make 2)
Begin at back leg. Using size 3.50 mm hook and col.A make 23 ch.
foundation row: 1 dc in 2nd ch from hook, 1 dc in each ch to end, turn. 22 dc.
row 2: 3 ch, 1 dc in 2nd ch from hook, 1 dc in next ch, 1 dc in each dc to end, turn. 24 dc.
row 3: 1 ch, 1 dc in each of 23 dc, 2 dc in last dc, turn. 25 dc.
row 4: 1 ch, 2 dc in first dc, 1 dc in each of 24 dc, turn. 26 dc.
row 5: 1 ch, 2 dc in first dc, 1 dc in each of 24 dc, 2 dc in last dc, turn. 28 dc.

row 6: 1 ch, 1 dc in first dc, 1 dc in each dc to end, turn.

row 7: 1 ch, 1 dc in each of 27 dc, 2 dc in last dc, turn. 29 dc.

row 8: as row 6.

Shape Back Leg

row 9: 1 ch, 1 dc in each of first 4 dc, 1 ss in next dc, fasten off. Leave next 6 dc, rejoin yarn to next dc, 1 dc in each of next 16 dc, 2 dc in last dc, turn.

row 10: as row 6. 18 dc.

row 11: 1 ch, 2 dc tog over first 2 dc, 1 dc in each of next 15 dc, 2 dc in last dc, turn. 18 sts.

row 12: as row 6.

rows 13–18: rep rows 11 and 12, 3 times.

Front Leg

row 19: 17 ch, 1 dc in 2nd ch from hook, 1 dc in each of next 15 ch, 1 dc in each of 17 dc, 2 dc in last dc, turn. 35 dc.

row 20: as row 6.

row 21: 1 ch, 1 dc in each of 34 dc, 2 dc in last dc, turn. 36 dc.

row 22: 1 ch, 2 dc in first dc, 1 dc in each of 35 dc to end, turn. 37 dc.

row 23: 1 ch, 2 dc in first dc, 1 dc in each of 35 dc, 2 dc in last dc, turn. 39 dc.

row 24: 1 ch, 2 dc in first dc, 1 dc in each of 38 dc to end, turn. 40 dc.

row 25: 1 ch, 1 dc in each of 39 dc, 2 dc in last dc, turn. 41 dc.

row 26: 1 ch, 2 dc in first dc, 1 dc in each of 40 dc to end, turn. 42 dc.

Shape Front Leg

row 27: 1 ch, 1 dc in each of first 4 dc, 1 ss in next dc, fasten off. Leave next 14 dc, rejoin yarn to next dc, 1 dc in each of next 21 dc, 2 dc in last dc, turn.

row 28: 1 ch, 2 dc in first dc, 1 dc in each of next 18 dc, turn leaving last 4 dc unworked. 20 dc.

row 29: miss first dc, 1 ss in next dc, 1 dc in each dc to last dc, 2 dc in last dc, turn. 19 dc.

row 30: 1 ch, 2 dc in first dc, 1 dc in each dc to last 3 dc, turn. 17 dc.

row 31: as row 29. 16 dc.

row 32: 1 ch, 2 dc in first dc, 1 dc in each dc to last 2 dc, turn. 15 dc.

rows 33 and 34: as rows 31 and 32. 13 dc.

row 35: miss first dc, 1 ss in next dc, 1 dc in each dc to end, turn. 11 dc.

row 36: 1 ch, 2 dc in first dc, 1 dc in each dc to last 2 dc, turn. 10 dc.

Shape Head

row 37: 1 ch, 2 dc in first dc, 1 dc in each dc to end, turn. 11 dc.

row 38: 1 ch, 1 dc in each dc to last dc, 2 dc in last dc, turn. 12 dc.

rows 39 and 40: as rows 37 and 38. 14 dc.

row 41: 1 ch, 1 dc in each of 12 dc, 2 dc tog over last 2 dc, turn. 13 sts.

row 42: 4 ch, 1 dc in 2nd ch from hook, 1 dc in each of next 2 ch (these 3 dc form the horn), 2 dc tog over next 2 dc, 1 dc in each of next 3 dc, 2 dc tog over next 2 dc. Fasten off.

HEAD GUSSET

Using size 3.50 mm hook and col.A make 2 ch.

row 1: 2 dc in 2nd ch from hook, turn.

row 2: 1 ch, 1 dc in first dc, 2 dc in last dc, turn. 3 dc.

row 3: 1 ch, 1 dc in each dc, turn.

rows 4–6: as row 3.

row 7: 1 ch, 2 dc in first dc, 1 dc in next dc, 2 dc in last dc, turn. 5 dc.

row 8: 1 ch, 2 dc in first dc, 1 dc in each of next 3 dc, 2 dc in last dc, turn. 7 dc.

rows 9–12: as row 3.

row 13: 1 ch, 2 dc tog over first 2 dc, 1 dc in each of next 3 dc, 2 dc tog over last 2 dc, turn. 5 sts.

row 14: 1 ch, 1 dc in each st to end, turn.

row 15: 1 ch, 2 dc tog over first 2 dc, 1 dc in next dc, 2 dc tog over last 2 dc, turn. 3 sts.

row 16: as row 14.

row 17: 1 ch, 2 dc tog over first 2 dc, 1 dc in last dc, turn. 2 sts.

row 18: 1 ch, 2 dc tog over rem 2 sts. Fasten off.

UNDERBODY

Using size 3.50 mm hook and col.A make 3 ch.

row 1: 1 dc in 2nd ch from hook, 1 dc in next ch, turn. 2 dc.

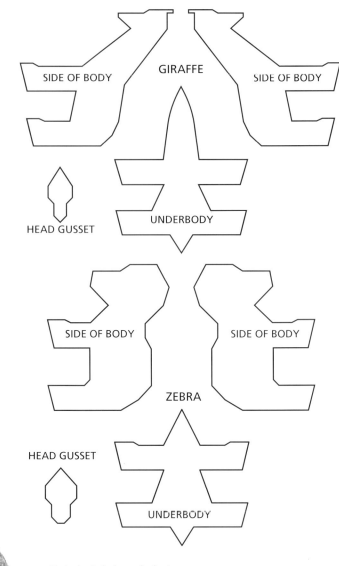

row 2: 1 ch, 1 dc in each dc, turn.

row 3: 2 dc in first dc, 1 dc in last dc, turn. 3 dc.

row 4: 1 ch, 2 dc in first dc, 1 dc in each dc to end, turn. 4 dc.

rows 5 & 6: as row 4. 6 dc.

row 7: 17 ch, 1 dc in 2nd ch from hook, 1 dc in each of next 15 ch, 1 dc in each dc to end, turn. 22 dc.

row 8: as row 7. 38 dc.

row 9: 1 ch, 1 dc in first dc, 1 dc in each dc to end, turn.

row 10: as row 9.

row 11: 1 ch, 2 dc in first dc, 1 dc in each dc to end, turn. 39 dc.

row 12: as row 11. 40 dc.

rows 13–15: as row 9.

Shape Back Legs

row 16: 1 ch, 1 dc in each of first 28 dc, turn leaving 12 dc unworked.

row 17: 1 ch, 2 dc tog over first 2 dc, 1 dc in each of next 14 dc, turn leaving 12 dc unworked.

row 18: 1 ch, 2 dc tog over first 2 dc, 1 dc in each dc to end, turn. 14 sts.

rows 19–24: as row 18. 8 sts.

rows 25 and 26: as row 9.

Front Legs

rows 27 & 28: as row 7.
4U dc.
rows 29 & 30: as row 9.
rows 31–34: as row 11.
44 dc.
row 35: as row 9.

Shape Front Legs

row 36: 1 ch, 1 dc in each of first 28 dc, turn leaving 16 dc unworked.
row 37: 1 ch, 1 dc in each of first 12 dc, turn leaving 16 dc unworked.
rows 38 & 39: as row 18. 10 sts.
rows 40–43: as row 9.
Rep rows 38–43 once more. 8 sts.
Rep rows 38–41 twice. 4 sts.
Rep rows 38 & 39 once again. 2 sts.
last row: 1 ch, 2 dc tog over 2 rem sts. Fasten off.

EARS (make 2)

Using size 3.50 mm hook and col.A make 5 ch.
row 1: 1 dc in 2nd ch from hook, 1 dc in each ch to end, turn. 4 dc.
row 2: 1 ch, 1 dc in first dc, 1 dc in each dc to end, turn.
row 3: as row 2.
row 4: 1 ch, 1 dc in first dc, 2 dc tog over next 2 dc, 1 dc in last dc, turn. 3 sts.
row 5: 1 ch, 2 dc tog over first 2 dc, 1 dc in last dc, turn. 2 sts.
row 6: 1 ch, 2 dc tog over 2 rem sts. Fasten off.

TO FINISH

Join Head Gusset to sides of head, matching lower point to end of nose. Leave horns protruding from top of head. Join centre back seam from top of head down to tail position, leaving an opening of about 10 cm (4 in) at centre to insert toy filling. Join from point of nose to corner beneath chin. Sew on Underbody with lower (short) point at end of centre back seam and upper (long) point beneath chin, matching sides of legs and gathering slightly across ends of feet.
Insert toy filling. Push filling into head and down to ends of legs with the blunt end of a pencil or similar tool. The toy should be very firmly filled. The firmer the filling, the better the giraffe will stand up. Close opening.
Sew Ears to top of head, folding lower edge of each at an angle so Ears stand up.

Embroidery

Use col.B to embroider circles of chain stitch following the photograph as a guide. Embroider a little smile in chain stitch, as illustrated.

Eyes

Bring col.B out at required position and secure with a small back stitch, then take several firm stitches through the head from one eye position to the other, pulling tightly to shape the head. Then work a french knot for each eye.

Tail

Cut 6 x 50 cm (19½ in) lengths of col.B and thread them through

seam at tail position, making 12 strands of equal length. Divide the strands into 3 groups of 4 and plait tightly for about 4 cm (1¾ in), then tie an overhand knot. Trim ends 2 cm (¾ in) below knot.

ZEBRA

SIDE OF BODY (make 2)

Begin at back leg. Using size 3.50 mm hook and col.A make 23 ch.
foundation row: 1 dc in 2nd ch from hook, 1 dc in each ch to end, turn. 22 dc.
row 2: 3 ch, 1 dc in 2nd ch from hook, 1 dc in next ch, 1 dc in each dc to end, turn. 24 dc.
Change to col.B. Work throughout in stripes of 2 rows col.B, 2 rows col.A. Carry the yarns up the side edge of the work except where instructed to fasten off. For a neat finish, when changing cols, work the last pull through of a row in the col. required for next row.
row 3: 1 ch, 1 dc in each dc to last dc, 2 dc in last dc, turn. 25 dc.
row 4: 3 ch, 1 dc in 2nd ch from hook, 1 dc in next ch, 1 dc in each of 24 dc, 2 dc in last dc, turn. 28 dc.
row 5: as row 3. 29 dc.
row 6: 1 ch, 2 dc in first dc, 1 dc in each dc to end, turn. 30 dc.
row 7: 1 ch, 2 dc in first dc, 1 dc in each dc to last dc, 2 dc in last dc, turn. 32 dc.
row 8: 1 ch, 1 dc in first dc, 1 dc in each dc to end, turn.
row 9: as row 3. 33 dc.
row 10: as row 8. Fasten off both cols.

Shape Back Leg

row 11: Leave first 11 dc, rejoin col.B to next dc, 1 ch, 1 dc in next dc, 1 dc in each dc to last dc, 2 dc in last dc, turn. 22 dc.
row 12: 1 ch, 1 dc in first dc, 1 dc in each dc to last 2 dc, 2 dc tog over last 2 dc, turn. 21 sts.
row 13: 1 ch, 2 dc tog over first 2 dc, 1 dc in each dc to end, turn. 20 sts.
rows 14–24: as row 8. Fasten off col.B.

Front Leg

row 25: (using col.A) 15 ch, 1 dc in 2nd ch from hook, 1 dc in each of next 13 ch, 1 dc in each dc to end, turn. 34 dc.
row 26: as row 8.
row 27: (join in col.B) 1 ch, 1 dc in first dc, 1 dc in each dc to last 2 dc, 2 dc tog over last 2 dc, turn. 33 sts.
row 28: 1 ch, 1 dc in 2 dc tog, 1 dc in each dc to last dc, 2 dc in last dc, turn. 34 sts.
rows 29 & 30: as row 8.
rows 31–34: as rows 27–30. 34 sts. Fasten off col.B.

Shape Front Leg

row 35: (using col.A) 1 ch, 1 dc in each of first 7 dc, 1 ss in next dc. Fasten off. Miss next 7 dc, rejoin col.B to next dc, 1 ch, 1 dc in each of next 17 dc to last dc, 2 dc in last dc, turn.
row 36: 1 ch, 2 dc in first dc, 1 dc in each dc to last 3 dc, 2 dc tog over next 2 dc, turn. 18 sts.
row 37: (join in col.A) 1 ch, 2 dc tog over first 2 sts, 1 dc in each dc to last dc, 2 dc in last dc, turn. 18 sts.
rows 38 & 39: as rows 36 & 37. 17 sts.
row 40: as row 36. 16 sts.

Shape Head

row 41: 1 ch, 2 dc in first dc, 1 dc in each dc to end, turn. 17 dc.

row 42: 1 ch, 1 dc in first dc, 1 dc in each dc to last dc, 2 dc in last dc, turn. 18 dc.

row 43: 1 ch, 2 dc in first dc, 1 dc in each dc to last dc, 2 dc in last dc, turn. 20 dc.

row 44: as row 42. 21 dc.

rows 45 & 46: as rows 41 & 42. 23 dc.

row 47: 1 ch, 1 dc in first dc, 1 dc in each dc to last 2 dc, 2 dc tog over last 2 dc, turn. 22 sts.

row 48: as row 8.

row 49: 1 ch, 2 dc tog over first 2 dc, 1 dc in each dc to last 2 dc, 2 dc tog over last 2 dc, turn. 20 sts.

Shape Nose

row 50: 1 ch, 2 dc tog over first 2 dc, 1 dc in each of next 8 dc, 1 ss in next dc, turn leaving 9 sts unworked, 1 ch, miss 1 ss, 1 dc in each of next 7 dc, 2 dc tog over next 2 sts, turn, 1 ch, 2 dc tog over first 2 sts, 1 dc in each of next 6 dc, 1 ss in 1 ch, 1 dc in each dc to last 2 dc, 2 dc tog over last 2 dc. Fasten off.

HEAD GUSSET

Using size 3.50 mm hook and col.B make 3 ch.

row 1: 1 dc in 2nd ch from hook, 1 dc in next ch, turn. 2 dc.

row 2: 1 ch, 1 dc in first dc, 1 dc in last dc, turn. Change to col.A. Work in stripes as for Back.

row 3: 1 ch, 2 dc in first dc, 2 dc in last dc, turn. 4 dc.

row 4: 1 ch, 1 dc in first dc, 1 dc in each dc to end, turn.

row 5: 1 ch, 2 dc in first dc, 1 dc in each dc to last dc, 2 dc in last dc, turn. 6 dc.

rows 6–8: as row 4.

row 9: as row 5. 8 dc.

rows 10–14: as row 4.

row 15: 1 ch, 2 dc tog over first 2 dc, 1 dc in each dc to last 2 dc, 2 dc tog over last 2 dc, turn. 6 sts.

row 16: 1 ch, 1 dc in 2 dc tog, 1 dc in each dc ending 1 dc in 2 dc tog, turn.

rows 17 & 18: as rows 15 & 16. 4 sts.

row 19: 1 ch, 2 dc tog over first 2 dc, 2 dc tog over last 2 dc, turn. 2 sts.

row 20: 1 ch, [1 dc in 2 dc tog] twice. Fasten off.

UNDERBODY

Using size 3.50 mm hook and col.B make 3 ch. Work in col.B throughout.

row 1: 1 dc in 2nd ch from hook, 1 dc in next ch, turn. 2 dc.

row 2: 1 ch, 1 dc in each of 2 dc, turn.

row 3: 1 ch, 2 dc in first dc, 1 dc in last dc, turn. 3 dc.

row 4: 1 ch, 2 dc in first dc, 1 dc in each dc to end, turn. 4 dc.

rows 5–8: as row 4. 8 dc.

Back Legs

row 9: 15 ch, 1 dc in 2nd ch from hook, 1 dc in

each of next 13 ch, 1 dc in each dc to end, turn. 22 dc.

row 10: as row 9. 36 dc.

row 11: 1 ch, 1 dc in first dc, 1 dc in each dc to end, turn.

row 12: as row 11.

row 13: 1 ch, 2 dc in first dc, 1 dc in each dc to end, turn. 37 dc.

row 14: as row 13. 38 dc.

rows 15–21: as row 11.

Shape Back Legs

row 22: 1 ch, 1 dc in first dc, 1 dc in each of next 26 dc, turn leaving 11 dc unworked.

row 23: 1 ch, 1 dc in first dc, 1 dc in each of next 15 dc, turn leaving 11 dc unworked. 16 dc.

row 24: 1 ch, 2 dc tog over first 2 dc, 1 dc in each dc to end, turn. 15 dc.

rows 25–31: as row 24. 8 dc.

rows 32–36: as row 11.

Front Legs

rows 37–48: as rows 9–20. 38 dc.

row 49: 1 ch, 1 dc in first dc, 1 dc in each of next 6 dc, 1 ss in next dc, fasten off. Leave next 5 dc, rejoin yarn to next dc, 1 ch, 1 dc in next dc, 1 dc in each dc to end. 24 dc.

row 50: as row 49. 10 dc.

rows 51 and 52: as row 11.

row 53: 1 ch, 2 dc tog over first 2 dc, 1 dc in each dc to end, turn. 9 dc.

row 54: as row 53. 8 sts.

Rep rows 51–54, 3 more times. 2 sts.

next row: 1 ch, 1 dc in each of 2 dc, turn.

foll row: 1 ch, 2 dc tog over 2 rem sts. Fasten off.

EARS (make 2)

Using size 3.50 mm hook and col.A make 7 ch.

row 1: 1 dc in 2nd ch from hook, 1 dc in each ch to end, turn. 6 dc.

row 2: 1 ch, 1 dc in first dc, 1 dc in each dc to end, turn.

rows 3–5: as row 2.

row 6: 1 ch, 1 dc in each of first 2 dc, 2 dc tog over next 2 dc, 1 dc in each of last 2 dc, turn. 5 sts.

row 7: 1 ch, 1 dc in first dc, 3 dc tog over next 3 sts, 1 dc in last dc, turn. 3 sts.

row 8: 1 ch, 3 dc tog over 3 rem sts. Fasten off.

MANE

Special Abbreviation: lp st: loop st, worked as follows: insert hook as directed, hold yarn in a loop over left forefinger, catch both threads below finger at base of loop and pull through, yrh, pull through 3 lps on hook, release the loop. The length of each loop is controlled by the forefinger (but where the loops will be cut to form a fringe, as below, this is not crucial).

Using size 3.50 mm hook and col.A make 31 ch.

row 1: 1 lp st in 2nd ch from hook, 1 lp st in each ch to last ch, 2 lp st in last ch, turn and work back along base of ch: 1 lp st in base of each ch to end. Fasten off.

TO FINISH

Join pieces and insert toy filling as given for Giraffe. Sew Mane along centre back seam beginning at top of head and ending at centre back. Pull gently on each loop to tighten it, then cut through and trim all the ends evenly to about 1.5 cm (½ in).

Eyes

Using size 3.50 mm hook and col.C make 3 ch and join into a ring with 1 ss in first ch made, (work over starting end) 6 dc into ring. Fasten off.

Pull gently on starting end to tighten centre. Sew one eye to each side of head, then use col.A to stitch between eyes and work french knots as given for Giraffe.

Using col.A work Tail as for Giraffe.

RABBIT CURTAIN

**TRY THE TRADITIONAL TECHNIQUE OF FILET CROCHET
WORKED FROM A CHART TO MAKE A PRETTY WINDOW DRESSING
FOR THE NURSERY.**

SIZE

Finished Panel to measure 60 x 85 cm (23½ x 33½ in) excluding
hanging loops. For a longer curtain, work extra Mesh Pattern
rows at the top, as required; for a wider curtain, work two or
more panels.

MATERIALS

3 x 100 g balls of Twilleys Lyscordet (4-ply cotton) in
col.78 White
2.00 mm and 2.50 mm hooks

TENSION

14½ mesh squares and 11½ rows to 10 cm (4 in) measured
over Mesh Pattern using size 2.50 mm hook.

PANEL

Using size 2.50 mm hook make 169 ch.
chart row 1 (foundation row): 1 tr in 5th ch from hook, * 1 ch,
miss 1 ch, 1 tr in next ch, rep from * to end, turn. 83 mesh squares,
as shown on row 1 of chart.
chart row 2: 2 ch, then read 2nd row of chart from left to right:
each blank square on the chart represents one mesh square, worked
as [1 ch, miss 1 ch, 1 tr in next tr]; each filled square on the chart
represents one block, worked as [1 tr in 1 ch sp, 1 tr in next tr],
work last tr in 3rd of 4 ch at beg row 1, turn.
chart row 3: 2 ch, then read 3rd row of chart from right to left, in
mesh pattern and blocks as before; where a mesh is worked above a
block, work [1 ch, miss 1 tr, 1 tr in next tr] and where a block is
worked above a block, work [1 tr in each of next 2 trs], work last tr
in 2nd of 3 ch at beg previous row, turn.
NOTE diagonal lines (for rabbit's whiskers and bird's beak) will be
embroidered later. Continue in this way, reading from successive
chart rows until chart row 94 is complete, or to length required.
Border
Change to size 2.00 mm hook.
round 1: 2 ch, 1 dc in first tr, * 1 dc in 1 ch sp, 1 dc in next tr, rep
from * to corner, ending [1 dc, 1 ch, 1 dc] in 2nd of 3 ch; work 2 dc
in side edge of each row to next corner, [1 dc, 1 ch, 1 dc] in base of
first ch, * 1 dc in 1 ch sp, 1 dc in base of next ch, rep from * along
lower edge to corner, ending [1dc, 1 ch, 1dc] in 2nd of 3 ch at
corner; 2 dc in side edge of each row, ending 1 ss in 2 ch sp at beg
of round.
round 2: 2 ch, 1 dc in 2 ch sp at corner, * 1 dc in each dc to corner,
[1 dc, 1 ch, 1 dc] in 1 ch sp at corner, rep from * ending 1 ss in

2 ch sp at beg of round.
Rep round 2, twice more.
First Strap
row 1: 1 ch, 1 dc in 2 ch sp at corner, 1 dc in each of next
6 dc, turn.
* row 2: 1 ch, 1 dc in each of next 7 dc, turn.
Rep this row until strap measures 7.5 cm (3 in) or length required to
fit curtain pole. Fasten off.
Second Strap
With right side of work facing, miss next 14 dc, rejoin yarn to next
dc, work as First Strap from * to end.
Make seven more straps in this way along top edge. Note that on
first row of last strap, last dc should be worked into 2 ch sp
at corner.
Edging
With right side of work facing, using size 2.00 mm hook, join yarn
to last dc of Border at top right hand corner of curtain, 1 ch, * 1 dc
in side edge of each row of strap to corner, 1 ch, fold strap towards
wrong side of curtain matching top edge to last row of Border, [1 dc
in next dc through both thicknesses] 7 times to next corner of strap,
1 ch, 1 dc in side edge of each row down to last row of Border,
ending 2 dc tog at corner; 1 dc in each of 14 dc along last row of
Border, ending 2 dc tog at base of next strap, rep from * along top
edge of work, ending 1 ss in 1 ch sp at corner of Border. Fasten off.
Embroider rabbit's whiskers and bird's beak as straight stitches.
Press as instructed on ball bands.

MESH PATTERN

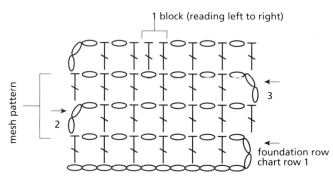

1 block (reading left to right)

mesh pattern

foundation row
chart row 1

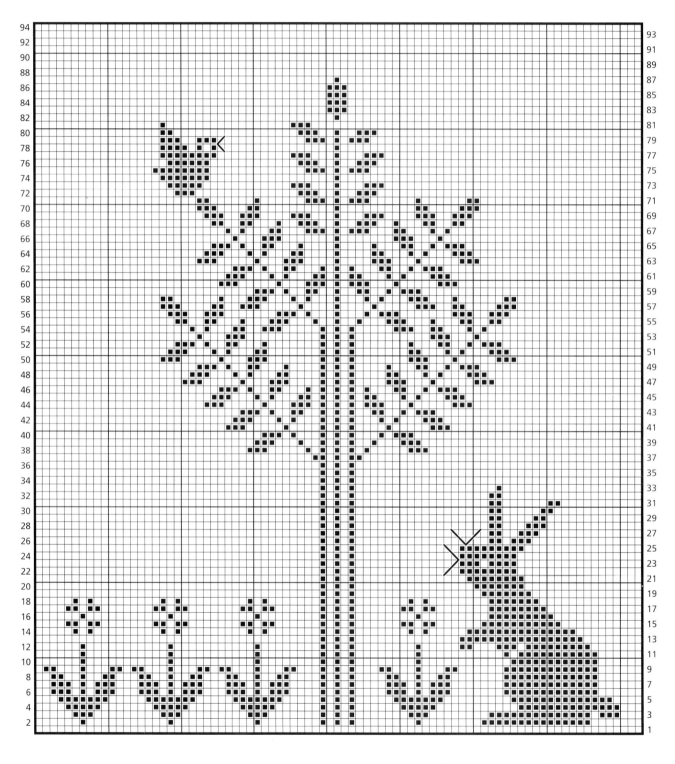

This design is completely reversible and looks good whichever way round you decide to hang it. The reverse of the curtain is shown on the right.

HEXAGON BLANKET

**WARM AND LIGHT, THIS SNUG DESIGN CAN EASILY BE ADAPTED
TO ANY SIZE REQUIRED.**

SIZE

64 x 78 cm (25 x 30½ in)
For a larger blanket, simply work more and/or longer strips. Note
that extra yarn will be required: approx.1 ball of A for every 17 extra
hexagons, and 1 ball of B for every 7 extra hexagons.

MATERIALS

2 x 50 g balls of Patons Fairytale DK in col.A (6302 Vanilla)
5 x 50 g balls of Patons Fairytale DK in col.B (6304
Peppermint)
3.50 mm and 4.00 mm hooks

TENSION

First hexagon made should measure 13 cm (5¼ in) from
corner to opposite corner. If your hexagon is too small,
try again with a larger hook; if it is too large, try a
smaller hook.
Tension is not crucial provided a change in size is
acceptable. However, if your tension is too loose, extra
yarn may be required.

Special Abbreviations: 2 dtr tog: [yrh twice, insert hook
as directed, yrh, pull through a lp, (yrh, pull through 2 lps)
twice] twice in same place, yrh, pull through 3 lps on hook.
3 dtr tog: [yrh twice, insert hook as directed, yrh, pull
through a lp, (yrh, pull through 2 lps) twice] 3 times in
same place, yrh, pull through 4 lps on hook.
1 rev dc: working from left to right (if you are right
handed): insert hook into next dc to right with hook facing
slightly downwards, catch yarn and pull through, turning
hook slightly back to the normal position; yrh, pull
through 2 lps on hook.

STRIP A (make 4)

FIRST HEXAGON

Using size 4.00 mm hook and col.A make 3 ch and join into a ring
with 1 ss in first ch made.
round 1: working over starting end: 6 dc into ring, 1 ss into first dc.
round 2: 3 ch, 2 dtr tog inserting hook in front lp only at base of
these 3 ch (first petal made), * 4 ch, 3 dtr tog inserting hook in front
lp only of next dc (second petal made), rep from * 4 more times,
4 ch, fasten off with 1 ss in top of first petal. Six petals made. Break
off col.A.
round 3: join col.B to back lp of dc behind first petal, 4 ch, 3 dtr in
same place, 4 dtr in back lp of next 5 dc, 1 ss in 4th of 4 ch at beg
of round.

HEXAGON PATTERN

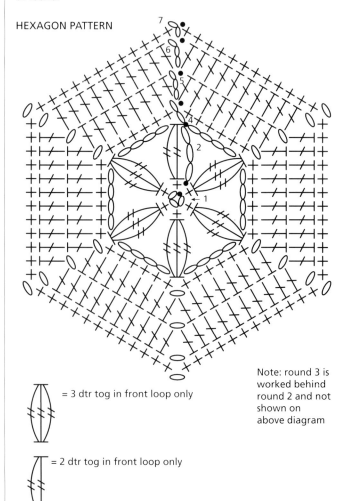

= 3 dtr tog in front loop only

= 2 dtr tog in front loop only

Note: round 3 is
worked behind
round 2 and not
shown on
above diagram

ound 4: 1 ss in top of first petal, 2 ch, 1 dc in same place as 1 ss, * [1 dc in 4 ch sp tog with next d tr behind] 4 times, (1 dc, 1 ch, 1 dc) in top of next petal, rep from * ending 1 ss in 2 ch sp at beg of round.

round 5: 3 ch, 1 tr in 2 ch sp at base of these 3 ch, * 1 tr in each of next 6 dc, (1 tr, 1 ch, 1 tr) in 1 ch sp, rep from * ending 1 tr in each of 6 dc, ss in 3 ch sp at beg of round.

round 6: 3 ch, 1 tr in 3 ch sp at base of these 3 ch, * 1 tr in each of next 8 tr, (1 tr, 1 ch, 1 tr) in 1 ch sp, rep from * ending join in col.A, 1 ss in 3 ch sp at beg of round. Break off col.B.

round 7: Continue in col.A: 2 ch, 1 dc in 3 ch sp at base of these 2 ch, * 1 dc in each of next 10 tr, (1 dc, 1 ch, 1 dc) in 1 ch sp, rep from * ending 1 ss in 1st of 2 ch at beg of round. Fasten off. Pull gently on starting end of yarn to tighten centre.

SECOND HEXAGON

Work as First Hexagon without fastening off. Join to First Hexagon as follows:

Place two hexagons side by side with RS uppermost and second hexagon made nearer to you. Insert hook in next 1 ch sp of nearer hexagon and out through corresponding 1 ch sp of hexagon above from back to front, yrh, pull lp through both ch sps and lp on hook (1 ss made). [Insert hook in back lp of next dc of nearer hexagon and out through back lp of next dc of hexagon above from back to front, yrh, pull lp through both sts and lp on hook (1 ss made)] 12 times. Work 1 ss joining next 2 corresponding ch sps. Fasten off. Work 3 more hexagons in the same way, joining them to form a strip of 5 as diagram 1.

STRIP B (make 3)

HALF HEXAGON

Using size 4.00 mm hook and col.A make 3 ch and join into a ring with 1ss in first ch made.

row 1: 1 ch, 4 dc into ring, turn.

row 2: 3 ch, [yrh twice, insert hook in front lp of dc at base of these 3 ch, yrh, pull through a lp, (yrh, pull through 2 lps) twice] twice in same place, yrh, pull through 3 lps on hook (first petal made), * 4 ch, 3 dtr tog inserting hook in front lp only of next dc (second petal made), rep from * twice more. (Four petals made.) Fasten off and turn the work.

row 3: with wrong side of work facing, join col.B to front lp of dc at base of last petal made, 4 ch, 2 dtr in same place, 4 dtr in front lp of each of next 2 dc, 3 dtr in front lp of next dc, turn.

row 4: 1 ch, 2 dc in top of first petal, miss first dtr, *[1 dc in 4 ch sp tog with next dtr behind] 4 times, (1 dc, 1 ch, 1 dc) in top of next petal, rep from * once more, [1 dc in 4 ch sp tog with next dtr behind] 4 times, 1 dc in top of last petal, 1 dc in same place tog with 4th of 4 ch at beg of previous row, turn.

row 5: 3 ch, 1 tr in first dc, * 1 tr in each of next 6 dc, (1 tr, 1 ch, 1 tr) in 1 ch sp, rep from * once more, 1 tr in each of next 6 dc, 2 tr in last dc, turn.

row 6: 3 ch, 1 tr in first tr, * 1 tr in each of next 8 tr, (1 tr, 1 ch, 1 tr) in 1 ch sp, rep from * once more, 1 tr in each of next 8 tr, 2 tr in 3rd of 3 ch at beg previous row. Fasten off.

row 7: with right side of work facing, join col.A to 3rd of 3 ch at beg row 6, 2 ch, 1 dc in same place as base of 2 ch, [1 dc in each of next 10 tr, (1 dc, 1 ch, 1 dc) in 1 ch sp] twice, 1 dc in each of next 10 tr, [1 dc, 1 ch, 1 dc] in last tr. Fasten off.

See diagram 2. Work 4 whole hexagons (as Second Hexagon of Strip A) and another Half Hexagon, joining them as shown.
Join the strips as shown in diagram 3:

Place two strips side by side with right sides uppermost. Join col.A to 1 ch sp of nearer strip at right hand side of seam. Insert hook in same ch sp and out through corresponding 1 ch sp of strip above from WS to RS, yrh, pull lp through both ch sps and lp on hook (1 ss made). * [Insert hook in back lp of next dc of nearer strip and out through corresponding lp above from back to front of motif, yrh, pull lp through both stitches and lp on hook (1 ss made)] 12 times. Work 1 ss joining next seam with corresponding ch sp. Rep from * all along the seam. Fasten off.

BORDER

1st round: With right side of work facing, using size 3.50 mm hook and col.A, join yarn to 1 ch sp at one corner of blanket, 2 ch, 1 dc in same 1 ch sp, work all round in dc as follows: along short sides, work 1 dc in each dc, 2 dc tog at each inner corner and [1 dc, 1 ch, 1 dc] in 1 ch sp at each outer point; along long sides, work 1 dc in each dc and ch sp of hexagons, and work 21 dc along side edge of each half hexagon (including 3 dc worked into centre ring). End round with 1 ss in 2 ch sp at beg of round.

2nd round: 1 ch, 1 dc in each dc of previous round, working 2 dc tog at inner corners and 2 dc in each 1 ch sp at outer points, ending 1 ss under 1 ch at beg of round.

3rd round: Without turning, work reverse dc from left to right (if you are right handed): 1 ch, 1 rev dc in each dc all round, missing 1 dc at each inner corner, ending 1 ss under 1 ch at beg of round. Fasten off.

Press as instructed on ball bands.

Diagram 3

Diagram 1 (Strip A)

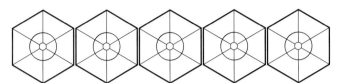

Diagram 2 (Strip B)

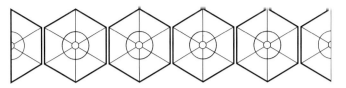

NURSERY CUSHION

SIMPLE SQUARES OF TREBLES AND BOLD APPLIQUÉ SHAPES, TRIMMED WITH EASY CHAIN STITCH EMBROIDERY.

SIZE

to fit cushion pad   45.5 x 45.5 cm (18 x 18 in)

MATERIALS

2 x 100 g balls of Sirdar Tropicana DK in
col.A (728 Watersprite)
1 x 100 g ball of Sirdar Tropicana DK in col.B (710 White)
1 x 100 g ball of Sirdar Tropicana DK in col.C (713 Dune)
3.50 mm hook
zip length 35.5 cm (14 in)
blunt-ended tapestry needle
darning needle
thin card

TENSION

18 sts and 9 rows to 10 cm (4 in) measured over Treble Pattern using size 3.50 mm hook. Tension is not crucial provided a change in size is acceptable, however if your tension is too loose extra yarn may be required.

RABBIT MOTIF

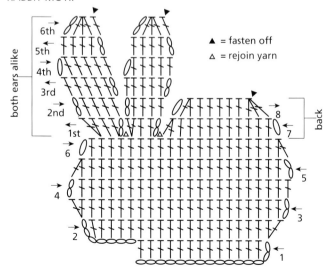

▲ = fasten off
△ = rejoin yarn

FRONT

RABBIT SQUARE (make 2)

Using size 3.50 mm hook and col.A make 35 ch.

foundation row (RS row): 1 tr in 3rd ch from hook, 1 tr in each ch to end, turn. 34 sts.

Treble Pattern

row 1 (WS row): 2 ch, miss first tr, 1 tr in each tr, ending 1 tr in 2nd of 2 ch, turn.

Rep this row 16 more times. 18 rows in all. Fasten off.

RABBIT (make 2)

Using size 3.50 mm hook and col.B make 15 ch.

row 1: 1 tr in 3rd ch from hook, 1 tr in each ch to end, turn. 14 sts.

row 2: 7 ch, 1 tr in 3rd ch from hook, 1 tr in each of next 4 ch, 1 tr in each tr ending 2 tr in 2nd of 2 ch, turn. 21 sts.

row 3: 2 ch, 1 tr in first tr, 1 tr in each tr ending 2 tr in 2nd of 2 ch, turn. 23 sts.

row 4: 2 ch, miss first tr, 1 tr in each tr ending 1 tr in 2nd of 2 ch, turn.

row 5: 2 ch, miss first tr, 1 tr in each tr to last tr and 2 ch, 2 tr tog over last 2 sts, turn. 22 sts.

row 6: 1 ch, miss 2 tr tog, 1 tr in each tr to last tr and 2 ch, 2 tr tog over last 2 sts. 21 sts.

diagram 1   diagram 2

chain stitch

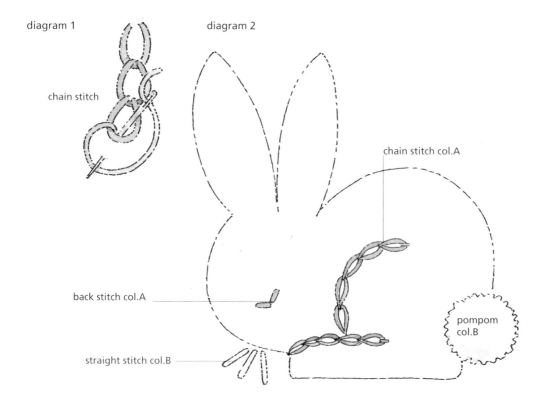

chain stitch col.A

back stitch col.A

straight stitch col.B

pompom
col.B

row 7: 1 ch, miss 2 tr tog, 1 tr in each of next 10 tr, 2 tr tog over next 2 tr, turn and complete back of rabbit as follows:

row 8: 1 ch, miss 2 tr tog, 2 tr tog over next 2 tr, 1 tr in each of next 5 tr, 3 tr tog over last 3 tr. Fasten off.

First Ear

Rejoin yarn to next tr at end of row 7.

1st row: 2 ch, 1 tr in tr at base of these 2 ch, 1 tr in next tr, 2 tr in next tr, turn. 5 sts.

2nd row: 2 ch, miss first tr, 1 tr in each of next 3 tr, 1 tr in 2nd of 2 ch, turn.

3rd row: 2 ch, 1 tr in tr at base of these 2 ch, 1 tr in each of next 3 tr, 1 tr in 2nd of 2 ch, turn. 6 sts.

4th row: 1 ch, miss first tr, 1 tr in each of next 4 tr, 1 tr in 2nd of 2 ch, turn.

5th row: 2 ch, miss first tr, 1 tr in each of next 4 tr, turn. 5 sts.

6th row: 2 ch, miss first tr, 3 tr tog over next 3 tr, 1 tr in 2nd of 2 ch. Fasten off.

Second Ear

Rejoin yarn to next tr at end of 1st row of First Ear.

Work 1st–6th rows as for First Ear.

With RS of Rabbit Squares facing, sew one rabbit to each square, facing in opposite directions as shown in photograph. Use a blunt-ended tapestry needle and col.B to work in back stitch around the edge of the motif without splitting the yarn. Using col.A, embroider outline of leg in chain stitch and closed eye in back stitch. Using col.B, embroider lines for whiskers in straight stitch.

(See diagrams 1 and 2.)

TAIL (make 2)

Cut 2 circles of card as shown in diagram 3. Place them together and wind with col.B as in diagram 4 until central hole is full. Insert point of scissors between the card layers and cut through strands all around edge. Tie a length of yarn firmly around the centre between the card circles, then snip away the card.

Sew one pompom tail to each rabbit.

diagram 3

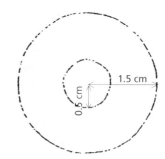

1.5 cm

0.5 cm

diagram 4

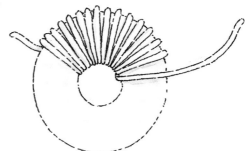

FLOWER SQUARE (make 2)

Using col.B work as given for Rabbit Square

FLOWER (make 6)

round 1: using size 3.50 mm hook and col.C make 4 ch and join into a ring with 1 ss in first ch made.

FLOWER

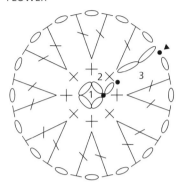

LEAF

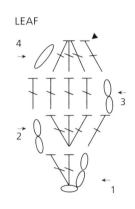

round 2: 1 ch, 8 dc into ring, 1 ss into first dc of round. 8 sts.
round 3: 3 ch, 1 tr in dc at base of these 3 ch, * 1 ch, [1 tr, 1 ch, 1 tr] in next dc, rep from * ending 1 ch, 1 ss in 2nd of 3 ch at beg of round. Fasten off.

LEAF (make 12)

Using size 3.50 mm hook and col.A make 3 ch.
row 1: 2 tr in 3rd ch from hook, turn. 3 sts.
row 2: 2 ch, miss first tr, 3 tr in next tr, 1 tr in 2nd of 2 ch, turn. 5 sts.
row 3: 2 ch, miss first tr, 1 tr in each of 3 tr, 1 tr in 2nd of 2 ch, turn.
row 4: 1 ch, miss first tr, 3 tr tog over next 3 tr, 1 tr in 2nd of 2 ch. Fasten off.
With RS of Flower Squares facing, arrange 3 Flowers on each Flower Square and sew in place as before. Using col.A, work a stem in chain stitch for each flower. Sew 6 leaves to each square in pairs as shown.
Arrange Squares as shown in diagram 5. Hold the top two squares with wrong sides together and use 3.50 mm hook to join col.C to top corner of right hand square, 1 ch, 1 dc in side edge of last

diagram 5 (Front)

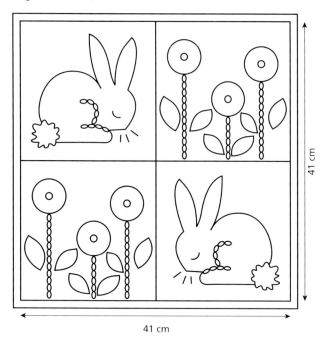

41 cm

41 cm

diagram 6 (Back)

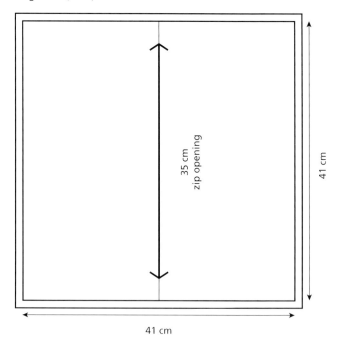

35 cm
zip opening

41 cm

41 cm

row of left hand square, 1 dc in next-to-last row of right hand square, *1 dc in next row of left hand square, 1 dc in next row of right hand square, rep from * ending 1 ss in lower corner of right hand square. Fasten off. Join the other two squares in the same way. Then join the two strips as follows: Place the two strips with WS together. Using size 3.50 mm hook join col.C to top of last tr at right hand corner of lower strip, 1 ch, 1 dc in sp between 1st and 2nd sts of upper strip, * miss 1 tr on lower strip, 1 dc in next tr, miss 2 trs on upper strip, 1 dc in next sp, rep from * all across ending 1 ss in last tr of lower strip. Fasten off.

BACK PANEL (make 2)
Using size 3.50 mm hook and col.A make 35 ch.
foundation row: 1 tr in 3rd ch from hook, 1 tr in each ch to end, turn. 34 sts.
Treble Pattern
row 1: 2 ch, miss first tr, 1 tr in each tr, ending 1 tr in 2nd of 2 ch, turn.
Rep this row 34 more times. 36 rows in all. Fasten off.
Place the two panels with WS together and join for about 2.5 cm (1 in) at each end of seam, leaving a 35.5 cm (14 in) opening for zip as diagram 6.
Work round zip opening as follows: with RS of work facing, using size 3.50 mm hook, join col.A to seam at one end of opening, 1 ch, 2 dc in side edge of each row to other end of opening, 2 dc tog at corner, 2 dc in side edge of each row down to first end, ending 1 dc tog with 1 ss in first dc made. Fasten off.
Tack the opening closed, matching row ends. Pin closed zip to wrong side of opening. Tack in place. Use col.A and darning needle to back stitch all round zip, just inside crochet edge. Undo tacking.

BACK BORDER
With RS of Back facing, use size 3.50 mm hook join col.C to last tr at top right hand corner.
round 1: 3 ch, 1 dc in tr at base of these 3 ch, 1 dc in each of next 33 sts, 1 dc in seam, 1 dc in each of next 34 sts to corner (69 dc along top edge), 2 ch, 2 dc in side edge of each row to corner (72 dc along 2nd side), 2 ch, 1 dc in base of each of 34 sts, 1 dc in seam, 1 dc in base of each of 34 sts (69 dc along lower edge), 2 ch, 2 dc in side edge of each of next 35 rows, 1 dc in side edge of next row, 1 ss in first of 3 ch (72 sts along 4th side).
round 2: 3 ch, 1 dc in 3 ch lp, work in dc along top edge, working [2 dc in 1 dc] 3 times evenly spaced; at corner, work [1 dc, 2 ch, 1 dc] in 2 ch sp; 1 dc in each dc down 2nd side, ending [1 dc, 2 ch, 1 dc] in 2 ch sp at corner; work along lower edge in same way as top edge, ending [1 dc, 2 ch, 1 dc] in 2 ch sp at corner; 1 dc in each dc up 4th side ending 1 ss in 1st of 3 ch. 74 sts along each side. Fasten off.

FRONT BORDER
Cut three 4 metre lengths of col.C and leave aside.
Using main ball of C, work as Back Border without fastening off. Place Front and Back with WS together.
next round: work through both thicknesses all round: 3 ch, 1 dc in both 2 ch sps, * 1 dc in each dc to corner, [1 dc, 2 ch, 1 dc] in both 2 ch sps, rep from * ending 1 ss in 1st of 3 ch.
edging round: double the three lengths of col.C and work 1 dc into 3 lps of yarn thus formed tog with next 2 ch sp, then complete the round working over the 6 yarn ends, pulling them gently every few sts for an even finish: 2 dc in same 2 ch sp, * 1 dc in each dc to corner, 3 dc in 2 ch sp, rep from * ending 1 ss in first dc of round. Fasten off. Trim the yarn ends to different lengths and run them in under the first few sts of last round to make a smooth join.
Press as instructed on ball bands.
Insert cushion pad.

SUPPLIERS

UK

PATONS WOOLS:
Coats Crafts UK
Tel: (01325) 394 237
Call for details of local stockists
and information on products
Website: www.coatscrafts.co.uk

ROWAN AND JAEGER:
Rowan Yarns
Rowan International
Green Lane Mill
Holmfirth
West Yorkshire
HD7 1RW
Tel: (01484) 681881
Fax: (01484) 687920
E-mail: rowanmail@rowanyarns.co.uk
Website: www.rowanyarns.co.uk
Worldwide distribution –
please phone for details of
your nearest stockist

SIRDAR YARNS:
Sirdar plc
Flanshaw Lane
Alverthorpe
Wakefield
W.Yorks
WF2 9JF
Tel: (01924) 371501

TEXERE YARNS:
College Mill
Barkerend Road
Bradford
BD1 4AU
Tel: (01274) 722191
Fax: (01274) 393500
Email: enquiries@texere-yarns.co.uk
Website: www.texere-yarns.co.uk
Mail order available

TWILLEYS:
Twilleys of Stamford
Roman Mill
Stamford
PE9 1BS
Tel: (01780) 752661
Fax: (01780) 765215
Website: www.tbramsden.co.uk

WENDY WOOLS:
Thomas B. Ramsden (Bradford) Ltd
Netherfield Road
Guiseley
Leeds LS20 9PD
Tel: (01943) 872264
Fax: (01943) 878689
Website: www.tbramsden.co.uk

Useful websites:

www.needlecraftfair.co.uk
Lists major suppliers and crochet
and knitting events

www.knitting-yarn.co.uk
Offers various yarns and equipment
at discount prices

www.knitwell.co.uk
On-line supplier of yarns

www.crochet.co.uk
Buy crochet supplies on-line

SOUTH AFRICA

Creative Kit Company
P.O Box 92043
Norwood
Johannesburg, 2117
Tel: (011) 640 6722
Fax: (011) 640 4016

Derlee Knitting Mills (Pty) Ltd
Jankelows Building
Jeppestown
Johannesburg, 2094
Tel: (011) 614 6038
Fax: (011) 614 0256

Knitting Wool Centre (Pty) Ltd
122 Victoria Road
Woodstock
Cape Town, 7925
Tel: (021) 447 1134
Fax: (021) 447 0289

Swansdon Knitting Wools (Pty) Ltd
8 Foundry Lane
Durban, 3001
Tel: (031) 304 0488
Fax: (031) 304 2047

United Wool (Pty) Ltd
32 A Mangold Street
Newton Park
Port Elizabeth, 6045
Tel: (041) 365 0735
Fax: (041) 365 0068

The Wool Shop
Shop 23, Hyperama Centre
Fleurdal
Bloemfontein, 9301
Tel: (051) 522 6553
Fax: (051) 447 0574

Wool & Hobby Centre (Pty) Ltd
21 A Chapman Building
Vanderbijlpark, 1911
Tel/Fax: (016) 933 4838

AUSTRALIA

Greta's Handcraft Centre
321 Pacific Highway
Lindfield
NSW 2070
Tel: (02) 9416 2489
Carry a large range of
Rowan Yarns and can give
further information
on stockists

Knitters of Australia
498 Hampton Street
Hampton
VIC 3188
Tel: (03) 9533 1233

Lincraft
Gallery level
Imperial Arcade
Pitt Street
Sydney
New South Wales 2000
Tel: (02) 9221 5111
Stores nationwide

Sunspun
185 Canterbury Road
Canterbury
VIC 3126
Tel: (03) 9830 1609
Mail Order
Distribute and carry a large
range of Rowan Yarns and
can give further information
on stockists

NEW ZEALAND

Knit World
Outlets nationwide
Auckland: (09) 837 6111
Tauranga: (07) 577 0797
Hastings: (06) 878 0090
New Plymouth: (06) 758 3171
Palmerston North: (06) 356 8974
Wellington: (04) 385 1918
Christchurch: (03) 379 2300
Dunedin: (03) 477 0400
Selected branches
stock Rowan wools

Spotlight Stores
Manukau: (09) 263 6760
or 0800 162 373
Wairau Park: (09) 444 0220
or 0800 224 123
Hamilton: (07) 839 1793
New Plymouth: (06) 757 3575
Wellington: (04) 472 5600
Christchurch: (03) 377 6121

INDEX

ACKNOWLEDGEMENTS

Special thanks to Sue Whiting.